A History of Agnostics in AA

Roger C

AA Agnostica

A History of Agnostics in AA

Library and Archives Canada Cataloguing in Publication

C., Roger, 1950-, author
A history of agnostics in AA / Roger C.

Includes bibliographical references.
Issued in print and electronic formats.

ISBN 978-0-9940162-5-6 (softcover). --ISBN 978-0-9940162-6-3 (ebook)

    1. Alcoholics Anonymous--History. 2. Alcoholism--Religious aspects. 3. Alcoholics--Rehabilitation. 4. Agnostics--Mental health. 5. Atheists--Mental health. 6. Twelve-step programs. I. Title.

HV5287.C78 2017   362.292'86   C2017-902118-4
                                             C2017-902119-2

Published in Canada by AA Agnostica
Cover design by Kyla Elisabeth
Interior layout and eBook version formatted by Chris G

Table of Contents

Preface

In case it is not clear early on, the author of this book, Roger C, has managed the website, AA Agnostica, since it was first created in mid-June 2011. The site is described as "a space for AA agnostics, atheists and freethinkers worldwide".

Two of the sixteen chapters are written by life-j. Over the years, he has written a number of articles about secular AA including one called "Open-minded" which was published in the October 2016 issue of the AA Grapevine, an issue devoted to "Atheist and Agnostic Members" of AA.

We do not claim to have written about every one of the individuals, groups, meetings, websites, conferences, etc. which have been a part of the history of agnostics in AA.

Roger C would especially like to thank all of the "non-believer" alcoholics he has met via AA Agnostica articles and comments, at the conventions in Santa Monica and Austin and in the rooms of AA. They have provided the "you are not alone" experience so crucial to long-term sobriety.

* IF YOU STRUGGLE W/
THE GOD BIT.
(AN INTERVENTIONIST DEITY)

THERE'S A MEETING FOR YOU

SECULAR AA MTG
(SPEC COMP GROUP
IE: LGBT / SPANISH)
MON 6 PM

UNITARIAN CHCH

SOLANA BEACH

2010: 60 SECULAR AA MTGS
2017: 320 " "

MAIN SOURCE OF
MY SOBRIETY

Introduction:
Time to Rally

INTOLERANCE OF INTOLERANCE, IS NOT TOLERANCE.

A few days ago I got an email from a woman, Emma. It was not at all an unusual email and followed a rather common motif. Emma had spent a bit of time reading various articles on the AA Agnostica website and wanted to know why we agnostics, atheists and free thinkers didn't start our own movement, our own organization.

She even suggested that we might not be real alcoholics.

After all, she insisted, "a common problem requires a common solution". And the solution to alcoholism was very clear: it was AA, as she understood it: the first 164 pages of *Alcoholics Anonymous*, the 12 Steps, God and "Conference-approved" literature.

If we agnostics didn't accept that, if that didn't work for us, then perhaps we were not real alcoholics and we were certainly not legitimate members of AA.

I replied with a brief email:

> My answer is simple, Emma. Tradition Three is very clear: "The only requirement for membership is a desire to stop drinking."
>
> And AA is meant to be a helping hand for any alcoholic who reaches out for help, and for that each AA member is responsible, according to our Responsibility Declaration.
>
> As for the solution, well, as Bill put it: "It must never be forgotten that the purpose of Alcoholics Anonymous is to sober up alcoholics. There is no religious or spiritual requirement for membership. No demands are made on anyone. An experience is offered which members may accept or reject. That is up to them." (Letter to Father Marcus O'Brien, written in 1943, and quoted in The Soul of Sponsorship by Robert Fitzgerald)
>
> If you don't understand or accept this, I really have nothing to add. If you want to impose a specific solution on people, well, AA is the wrong place for that.

HEALTHY HUMAN CONNECTION

1

...tion was over. She had shared her understanding of AA. ...my understanding of AA. We were not going to come to ...t; that was certain.

...king though. About AA and the 12 Steps and God. And about another quote from the co-founder of AA, Bill Wilson:

> *In AA's first years I all but ruined the whole undertaking... God as I understood Him had to be for everybody. Sometimes my aggression was subtle and sometimes it was crude. But either way it was damaging – perhaps fatally so – to numbers of non-believers. (Grapevine Article, "The Dilemma of No Faith", 1961)*

And that led me to question whether AA had become more inclusive over the past eight decades. Specifically, had Alcoholics Anonymous become more accepting towards non-believers since Bill W wrote about his aggression and the perhaps fatal consequences that might have been its result?

What could our Fellowship do to be more accommodating of we alcoholics who attribute our sobriety to an inner resource (Appendix II of the Big Book) rather than to a Higher Power, whom many in AA choose to call "God"?

Big questions.

"God", I thought (pun intended), "It would take a book to answer those questions!"

And so here's the book.

A History of Agnostics in AA has actually been in the works for the past six years. A much shorter version was published in 2011. At the time, my home group had been booted out of Intergroup in Toronto and I thought it would be helpful to find out how agnostics had been treated over the years in AA. The research could be done online and it would take – what – a weekend or two?

It would take three full months. Very little information about we agnostics in AA had been written, recorded or preserved anywhere. With the support of some wonderful people – specifically William White, the author of *Slaying the Dragon: A History of Addiction Treatment and Recovery in America*, Ernie Kurtz, the author of *Not-God: A History of Alcoholics Anonymous* and Michelle Mirza, the Chief Archivist at the AA General Service Office in New York – a 27 page essay called "A History of Agnostic Groups in AA" was put together and published online in September 2011.

This book contains most everything that was in that essay. And much more, including information shared over the years in articles posted on AA Agnostica.

And this book is divided into three main parts.

The first part is called **Our History**. It begins with a bit of an overview, "An Agnostic in AA", and then recounts our early history beginning with Jim Burwell, one of the very first agnostics in AA, and moves on to the launching of the first agnostic meetings in cities like Chicago, Los Angeles and New York.

It also deals with the not uncommon and relatively recent "rejection" of agnostic groups and meetings, by Intergroups in Canada and the United States. It has a chapter on "Changing the 12 Steps", as they were written and published in 1939, as that issue has often generated controversy. Finally, Part One deals in some detail with the expulsion of agnostic groups by the Greater Toronto Area Intergroup and how this matter was brought before a human rights tribunal and ultimately resolved.

The next part is about **Problems in AA**. There are a few of these for we agnostics, atheists and free thinkers. First, we look at "special composition groups" such as women, black and young people and the LGBTQ community for two important reasons: so that we secularists in AA understand that we are not alone in sometimes being treated as outcasts and in order to understand how the problems faced by these groups were dealt with by AA, both at the local level and by the General Service Office. Also discussed is the emergence of religious movements within the Fellowship as well as some characteristics of conventional AA, such as its religiosity and tendencies towards conformity. Finally we write about the lack of "Conference-approved" literature by, about and for non-believers in AA, in spite of efforts to produce such literature that go back to the 1970s.

As it should and must be, the third and final part of the book is called **Moving Forward**. We begin by looking at the explosion of "Non-Conference-approved" literature for non-believers in AA. We then have chapters about our first two conventions, in Santa Monica, California and Austin, Texas and, in a chapter between these two, "Progress not perfection", we admit to having had our own imperfections in the planning and organization of these two remarkable and historical conventions. The final chapters deal with the growth of our secular movement in AA and "Who We Are".

The appendices contain secular versions of "How It Works" as well as the histories of the launch and growth of ten secular groups in Canada. In 2009 there was one agnostic group in Canada while today there are twenty-five in five different provinces. The stories of these groups engage and inform in an encouraging sort of way. A third appendix shares a few articles originally posted on AA Agnostica.

The whole book is all about two things. First is the identification of the problems faced by we agnostics, atheists and freethinkers in AA. And these can be broken down into one simple fact: we don't attribute our sobriety to a supernatural Higher Power. Nor need we in AA. Read Tradition Three. And as Bill W put it, "All people must necessarily rally to the call of their own particular convictions and we of AA are no exception. All people should have the right to voice their convictions." (General Service Conference, 1965)

And second, the book is about how these problems could and should be dealt with as our secular movement gains momentum within AA. There is no longer a "fake it until you make it" approach to being a non-believer in AA. That's over. That's history. Let us all acknowledge that "To thine own self be true" is a healthy and essential approach to long term sobriety.

It's time to rally.

And we shall rally to the call of our own particular convictions and we shall do that within our AA Fellowship.

Part One:
Our History

Chapter 1:
An Agnostic in AA

I went to my first AA meeting when I was in rehab back in 2010. It was a speaker meeting and there was a fellow on stage who talked about how he owed his sobriety to "the Guy in the sky".

I thought, "Are you kidding me?" But, of course he wasn't. I was soon to discover that there was a lot of God talk at AA meetings. That is the first thing that bothers we agnostics and atheists in AA.

I should say that I am not speaking for all agnostics and atheists in AA. Nobody can do that. But as the editor of the website **AA Agnostica**[1] for the last six years and having been heavily involved in secular AA meetings, I am in contact with many agnostic members and know that many of them feel and react much the same as I do.

But back to the God talk: the God that is talked about at meetings is often a Christian God, an anthropomorphic (created in man's image – "Father", "He" or "Him") and interventionist (who can solve a problem with alcohol "if He were sought") supernatural being.

That doesn't work for me or other atheist alcoholics.

Most of us believe that what works in AA to keep us sober are two things: first, tapping an "inner resource" (see Appendix II of the Big Book) that makes us strive to be sober, and better, human beings. And, second, the fellowship. Going to an AA meeting and talking with others who understand the problem of alcoholism is a wonderful form of group therapy. The support of others (Step 12) plays a key part in our recovery, according to our more secular AA members, not a God.

The God talk might even be tolerable except for one thing and that is our second problem: we agnostics in AA are often not allowed to be honest at "traditional" AA meetings and even suggest that we personally don't believe in this God. There is apparently an unofficial policy in Alcoholics Anonymous for non-believers at AA meetings that might well be called: "Don't Tell".

And if you do talk about your lack of belief, you will often be subjected to a rebuttal, or an outright attack. It is one place at an AA meeting where crosstalk will sometimes happen. Or you will be confronted after the meeting. When that first happened to me I was stunned. You see, I have a Masters degree and spent years at McGill University working on my doctorate in Religious Studies. I taught ordinands (women and men studying to be church ministers). I was the "resident atheist" at the Faculty of Religious Studies and was treated with genuine respect. Not so much in AA. Many agnostics and atheists are treated with disrespect in AA, if not outright contempt.

That's a real problem.

And the last, the third problem, that many of us experience in AA are meetings that end with the Lord's Prayer. To say that AA is "spiritual not religious" and then recite the Lord's Prayer, well, that just doesn't wash. The Lord's Prayer is found in the New Testament in the Gospel of Matthew (6:5-13) with a shorter version in the Gospel of Luke (11:1-4). It was said to have been taught by Jesus to his disciples and is considered the essential summary of the gospels, of the religion of Christianity.

Because it discriminates against those with other beliefs or with no religious beliefs at all, the Lord's Prayer was eliminated from public schools by the Supreme Court in the United States in 1962. And in 1988, the Ontario Court of Appeal ruled that the "recitation of the Lord's Prayer, which is a Christian prayer... impose(s) Christian observances upon non-Christian pupils and religious observances on non-believers" and thus constitutes a violation of the freedom of conscience and religion provisions in the Charter of Rights and Freedoms. That was the end of the Lord's Prayer in public schools in Canada.

Agnostics and atheists believe that the Lord's Prayer does not belong at AA meetings. It's fine at a religious church meeting but to say that AA is "spiritual but not religious" and then end a meeting with the Lord's Prayer is a real contradiction.

After getting out of rehab, I went to a lot of AA meetings. And it got to the point where I just couldn't stand them. Too much of the "God bit". I realized I could no longer go to them and I was terrified I would start drinking again.

But, almost accidentally, I went one Saturday to my first ever agnostic AA meeting: Beyond Belief, in Toronto. It was, for me, a superb meeting.

When I got out I threw my hands up in the air and I shouted, "I'm saved!"

I have been going to secular AA meetings ever since. There was only that one meeting for non-believers in AA in Canada in the summer of

2010, when I went to Beyond Belief. Today there are more than twenty-five in five provinces. These secular meetings are now growing with great momentum.

These secular AA meetings – without any doubt at all – have been the main source of my sobriety. I know and feel that "I am not alone" and that I am free to express any doubts or disbeliefs I may have and that I can be totally honest.

For me, as for many other agnostics in AA, it's the fellowship that makes the difference. It's the frequent "remember when" stories that help to keep me from going back. It's learning so much from others about how they are able to deal with their alcoholism and to maintain their sobriety, truly, "one day at a time". It's the understanding, caring and support of the people at these AA meetings. Back in rehab, and in my early days and months of recovery, the word "gratitude" meant nothing to me at all.

Today I experience it every single day.

AA is meant to be here for all who reach out for help. We are a "kinship of universal suffering" as Bill Wilson put it and we need to let everyone who attends an AA meeting know and feel that they are welcome, regardless of belief or lack of belief.

[1] **AA Agnostica**: http://aaagnostica.org/

Chapter 2:
Rejection

Two agnostic groups – We Agnostics and Beyond Belief – were booted off of the official list of AA group meetings in the Greater Toronto Area (GTA) on May 31, 2011.

This was done by the GTA Intergroup.

Beyond Belief had been around for more than a year and a half. Twelve people attended its first meeting on September 24, 2009. It was, officially, the first agnostic AA group in Canada. We Agnostics had its first meeting almost a year later, on September 7, 2010. And both meetings were growing. To give more people an opportunity to participate, Beyond Belief had recently added a second weekly meeting on Saturdays.

The GTA Intergroup passed a motion that the two groups "be removed from the meeting books directory, the GTA AA website, and the list of meetings given over the phone by Intergroup to newcomers." The motion passed 24 to 15 with 9 abstentions.

The groups were also excluded from participating in, and voting at, the regular monthly Greater Toronto Area Intergroup (GTAI) meetings.

The next day, on Wednesday, I emailed the Toronto Star newspaper and later that day talked to a reporter, Leslie Scrivener. Later that weekend an article appeared on the front page of the Toronto Star. On the very top of the front page. The title was perfect, **Does religion belong at AA? Fight over 'God' splits Toronto AA groups.**[1] It came with a picture of a Catholic Priest in a church, Reverend Peter Watters, 50 years sober, who claimed that "belief in a higher power, God, is essential to getting sober in Alcoholics Anonymous".

Individual vs. group conscience

Many might consider contacting the Toronto Star a taboo. It has been argued that it was a violation of Traditions One and Ten. And it has also been argued that it was solely up to the group conscience – of either or both of the evicted groups – to decide how to deal with their expulsion.

Tradition One states: "Our common welfare should come first, personal recovery depends upon AA unity". Tradition One was indeed violated, and that was done by the GTA Intergroup.

Our common welfare should without a doubt come first, and it includes the welfare of agnostics, atheists and freethinkers. It is appalling – the word "sinful" jumps to mind – that Intergroup didn't understand this basic AA principle. But clearly it didn't.

Tradition Ten states: "Alcoholics Anonymous has no opinion on outside issues; hence the AA name ought never be drawn into public controversy".

To begin with, the expulsion of these groups was not an outside issue. Clearly, it was an inside issue.

And it was not an issue that could be allowed to be buried in the basement of a church. There are standards that AA has to meet, and not just standards within our fellowship. The Ontario Human Rights Code, adopted in 1962, prohibits discrimination based upon an individual's beliefs, or lack thereof, and goes on to say that this principle "extends to situations where the person who is the target of such behaviour has no religious beliefs whatsoever, including atheists and agnostics".

Was Intergroup violating basic human values, fundamental human rights?

A good question. An important question.

Finally, the question is raised as to whether or not dealing with this expulsion should have been left to the conscience of the two groups.

But I, too, have a conscience. Every human has a conscience. And perhaps the most important part of a person is his or her conscience: how she or he feels about the world and what is right or wrong in it. And that too needs to be acknowledged. And respected. To do otherwise is wrong and invariably a part of authoritarianism.

When my home group was booted out of the AA Intergroup, my conscience screamed at me to act. To act immediately. As noted earlier, I was determined that this would not be an issue buried in a church basement. Any delay in a response was going to be a problem that would further hurt those already victimized. And so I acted.

And I have no doubt that it was the right thing to do.

Fallout

On Thursday, I went to the evening meeting of my home group Beyond Belief, one of the two groups booted out of the Greater Toronto Area Intergroup (GTAI).

There were, as usual, some thirty people present. They were, to put it mildly, broken hearted. There was a fear in the room that the group and the meeting were as good as dead. If it did not die immediately it would wither away over time. After all, we were not now on any lists.

"Where will I go?" "But I love this meeting!" "They hate us." "What am I going to do now?" That was the mood as I entered the room.

Some were crying. One of them was a wonderfully talented Canadian actress. I had sat beside her and chatted with her at her first Beyond Belief meeting, some six months earlier. After that first meeting she had given me a big hug and told me, "Roger I have a new home!" Now her head was on the table and she sobbed uncontrollably.

Joe C, the author of *Beyond Belief: Agnostic Musings for 12 Step Life* and one of the co-founders of the group Beyond Belief, described the expulsion of his group this way:

> *I was crushed by Toronto Intergroup's decision. I grew up in AA. I have been sober since I was a teenager. I have always been outrageous. I have always pushed the envelope. I have always been tolerated and loved. When I was told that I was no longer welcome here it was an innocence lost that I cannot properly express. It was like having my family tell me to leave and never come back. For weeks, I was flabbergasted. I was angry and I was hurt.*

Larry K, one of founders of We Agnostics, the other group booted out, put it this way:

> *The decision prompted tears and shock among the three dozen or so people who had embraced the secular groups. "It was painful. It's shunning," said Knight. "It was unbelievable that an organisation that can't kick anybody out, and that prides itself on that, had kicked us out."*

The action taken by the GTA Intergroup was extreme. But let us be clear: there has always been tension between agnostics and the

Christian members of Alcoholics Anonymous. What happened at the Intergroup meeting in that church basement in Toronto merely exposed a long-festering wound within AA.

So, what's it all about, dear friends? Why did they do it? Why did Intergroup boot the two agnostic groups out?

We shall return to this topic in due course but first, well, we need some history.

[1] **Does religion belong in AA? Fight over 'God' splits Toronto AA groups**: http://aaagnostica.org/wp-content/uploads/2016/08/ Toronto-Star-Article-2011.pdf

Chapter 3:
The "God Bit"

The "God" part in the 12 Steps comes from Bill Wilson. The rest of it, "as we understood Him", was Jim Burwell's contribution.

But let's start at the beginning...

AA's soon-to-be co-founders met on May 12, 1935 (Mother's Day), with Bill trying to help Dr. Bob sober up at Dr. Bob's home in Akron, Ohio. Wilson worked away at that for almost a month: it would historically turn out to be one of the most significant recorded examples of one drunk helping another. Dr. Bob took his last drink on June 10, 1935 (a beer to steady his hand for surgery), and this is generally accepted as the founding date of AA.

In January of 1938, Jim Burwell joined the fellowship. AA consisted of two groups: one in Akron and the other one in New York. The latter group held one meeting a week, at Bill's home in Brooklyn, which was attended by six or eight men. Only three men in that group, including Bill, had been sober more than a year. AA was a fledgling organization, to say the least.

Bill and Bob were both members of a Christian revivalist movement, the Oxford Group. "The early meetings were quite religious, in both New York and Akron. There was always a Bible on hand, and the concept of God was all biblical," Jim reported.

Into that mix came Jim, "their self-proclaimed atheist, completely against all religion".

Jim presented quite a challenge to the group, as he later wrote in *Sober for Thirty Years*. "I started fighting nearly all the things Bill and the others stood for, especially religion, the 'God bit.' But I did want to stay sober, and I did love the understanding Fellowship."

At one point, his group held a prayer meeting to decide what to do with him. "The consensus seems to have been that they hoped I would either leave town or get drunk."

Jim was part of a big battle which took place in 1939 over *Alcoholics Anonymous, The Story of How More Than One Hundred Men Have Recovered from Alcoholism* (the name of the 1939 edition), commonly known as the Big Book.

Thanks to Jim, two key changes were made: First, the word "God" was changed to "God as we understood Him" in two of the 12 Steps.

Second, and most importantly, the word "suggested" was added to the phrase: "Here are the steps we took, which are 'suggested' as a program of recovery."

It is impossible to even try to explain how important that word has been over the years.

There is no question that Bill came to very much appreciate the contribution of Jim Burwell and the other atheists and agnostics in early AA. As he put it they "had widened our gateway so that all who suffer might pass through, regardless of their belief or lack of belief."

But was the gateway widened enough? Looking back some eight decades after the humble beginnings of Alcoholics Anonymous, the question has to be asked.

Indeed, the divisions in AA at the time were significant, and they do reflect current problems within the fellowship.

Robert Thompson's biography, *Bill W.*, written in 1975, touches on these problems as he describes the late 1930s meetings at Bill Wilson's home in Brooklyn:

> *There were agnostics in the Tuesday night group, and several hardcore atheists who objected to any mention of God. On many evenings Bill had to remember his first meeting with Ebby. He'd been told to ask for help from anything he believed in. These men, he could see, believed in each other and in the strength of the group. At some point each of them had been totally unable to stop drinking on his own, yet when two of them had worked at it together, somehow they had become more powerful and they had finally been able to stop. This, then – whatever it was that occurred between them – was what they could accept as a power greater than themselves. (p. 230)*

Many of the nonbelievers in this new century are not at all comfortable with the language of the Big Book or of the 12 Steps, language which pre-dates World War II.

And so it is asked, today: What about this "God bit"?

Jim Burwell went on to start AA groups in Philadelphia, Baltimore, and San Diego. Among the first ten members of the fellowship on the East Coast, he is often considered the third founder of AA. Jim is the first agnostic AA member to die sober: His sobriety date was June 15, 1938, and he died on September 8, 1974.

Chapter 4:
Early History

Chicago

Our movement – the growth of secular meetings within AA – began, ironically enough, in a church, the Unitarian Universalist Church.

And it was started by a guy by the name of Wilson, but not Bill, Don Wilson.

Don was a member of the Unitarian Universalist Church and had been for a number of years. He had first joined in his mid-teens, in his home town of Omaha, Nebraska. "I joined this church free of dogma or creed, and have ever since shared in the music-making and the Sunday services of one or another Unitarian-Universalist congregation."

He was also an alcoholic and a member of AA.

It hadn't always been easy for Don. In the early sixties he had tried AA and had attended meetings for six months but left, put off by all the religiosity. "I was unable to work it, because of the religious language in which the 12 steps are couched," he said.

He came back a decade later. His drinking had almost killed him. This time he decided he had to tough it out, no matter how hard.

After about four years of sobriety, in the autumn of 1974, he gave a talk at the Second Unitarian Church on Barry Street on the topic, "An Agnostic in AA: How it Works for Me".

The talk was well received by the congregation, and he ended up delivering it in several Unitarian churches. In fact, one of the ministers encouraged him to start an AA meeting especially for atheists and agnostics.

The first ever meeting in AA explicitly for nonbelievers was held on January 7, 1975.

In Chicago. In a church.

And thus was born Quad A: Alcoholics Anonymous for Atheists and Agnostics (AAAA).

Don not only founded the group in Chicago, but he also played a role in starting the Quad A groups in Evanston and Oak Park.

On February 22, 1995, The Chicago Tribune published an article with the headline, **A Different Road: Quad A Offers Help to Alcoholics Who Don't Buy Into God.**[1] It begins like this:

> *Six o'clock Saturday night and the drunks are having a party.*
>
> *This is news?*
>
> *It is when the party is in Chicago's Second Unitarian Church on Barry Street. The drunks are sober, and the party is to commemorate the 20th anniversary of a controversial 12-step recovery group - Alcoholics Anonymous (AA) for Atheists and Agnostics, known in AA circles as Quad A (AAAA).*

A brief history of Quad A in Chicago, it ends most appropriately:

> *"These (12) steps are but suggestions," the early AA members wrote in Alcoholics Anonymous, dubbed "The Big Book" in AA circles, but inevitably a churchlike push for orthodoxy began in some quarters. Perhaps it was just as inevitable that a group for atheists, agnostics, humanists, free spirits and "bad attitudes" would be created for those who wanted sobriety without conformity.*

More than 30 years after the first ever AA meeting for non-believers, a Quad A Unity Conference was held on September 13, 2009, in Chicago. More than a hundred people attended. By their very presence, they were able to "bear witness to the reality that there are hundreds of atheists and agnostics who are working the program and staying sober," Chuck K, principal organizer of the event, told those in attendance in his welcoming remarks.

The Conference also came with a sixteen page leaflet which contained the Conference schedule and included other terrific speakers. It had an article about Don Wilson, "A Man of Distinction". It contained a copy of the 1995 article written in the Chicago Tribune, "A Different Road". It also contained several versions of secular Steps and in the end it described AA in eight words, organized as four times two words. The first two words were "Quit Drinking". The second two words "Trust AA". The third two words "Clean House". And the last two words "Help Others".

A pretty simple understanding of AA.

The keynote address was delivered by Lisa D, and it was called, "How a Humanist Works the AA Program".

Lisa described how she had come to understand that human values – "empathy, compassion, integrity, mindfulness, honesty, open-minded-ness, diligence, excellence, serenity, courage, wisdom, and of course intimacy" – were the "greater power" to which she must strive to align herself.

Her talk was about how she worked the 12 Steps. Humanists, athe-ists, agnostics, secularists work the 12 Steps and, like everybody else following the suggested AA program of recovery, each does it according to his or her belief or *lack of belief*.

Early in her talk, Lisa expresses her gratitude that "the very first meet-ings I ever attended were Quad A". Otherwise, if she had heard the God bit in her early attempts at sobriety she might have "run out the door screaming" and picked up again.

The "Man of Distinction", Don Wilson, hadn't been so lucky. There were not any such meetings when he stumbled, and was back out for a decade. However, having stumbled, having picked himself up, he started the first ever group and meeting explicitly for agnostics and atheists.

He defined his agnosticism very simply: "I could never believe in a God small enough to fit inside my head."

And it is also clear that without him Quad A would not have been born.

Chuck K, the organizer of the Quad A Unity Conference mentioned earlier, reported at the We Agnostics and Atheists Conference in Austin in 2016 (more on this later) that Don was both a musician and he also loved to play cards. He became very well known within Chicago AA because of his reputation as a card player and musician. He was also a very sociable and outgoing guy.

The Quad A meetings were not listed in the Chicago AA directory until the 1980s, more than five years after they had been launched. A lawyer, John K, pushed for that and wanted them listed, but the Central AA Office was reluctant to list these groups. "This is Don's group," he told them. And so as Chuck reported: "Everybody knew

Don and so the atheist / agnostic group became Don's group in the minds of many of the people who were in the Central Office. The next directory, there we were. Officially listed AA, Quad A: Alcoholics Anonymous for Atheists and Agnostics".

Don expired with the old millennium. Fittingly, a memorial service was held for him at the Second Unitarian Church.

Today Quad A is going strong. There are thirteen meetings in Chicagoland. They are listed by the Chicago Intergroup and in fact one of the search options when you are looking for a meeting on the Chicagoland Intergroup site is called "Atheist / Agnostic". So you can actually look for those secular meetings in Chicago.

Los Angeles and Austin

"I am the daddy of all the 'We Agnostics' groups!"

The man who spoke those words, Charlie Polacheck, died on February 27, 2012, at the age of 98. They are ten words that no other human being could have ever uttered, which places them in a rather unique category.

And Charlie may indeed have at least partial ownership of the "We Agnostics" brand in Alcoholics Anonymous.

He co-founded the very first AA group ever to be called "We Agnostics," in 1980 in Los Angeles. Of course the name "We Agnostics" is also a chapter in the Big Book.

When I talked to Charlie, he was quite surprised. I told him that I was writing an article "A History of Agnostic Groups in AA" and his response was almost a shriek: "Really!" It was so exciting to him that we go public on this. It was so exhilarating to him that this would cease to be a secret within AA.

The other co-founder, Megan D, was new to sobriety. She remembers starting the group with Charlie:

> *I got sober on Jan. 1, 1980. My first regular meeting took place immediately. I met Charlie about a month later. We spoke of our mutual atheism and he told me there were many of us in the program, but that we kept a low profile. About three months later he came to me and asked me to help him start a meeting for people like us. We were so cute trying to decide what to call*

ourselves. We finally decided to name our meeting after Chapter 4 of the Big Book.

At the time Charlie was 66 years old and had been sober in AA for nine years. "I was a nonbeliever and I felt that it was only fitting and proper to have a meeting which was friendly to nonbelievers."

According to Nick H, the chair of the host committee for the We Agnostic and Atheists Conference in Austin, Texas in 2016, Charlie was fooled into attending his first AA meeting by his wife. "He went and he was horrified", Nick reported. It was at a Catholic Church and it was full of God stuff and Charlie told a friend that "I am never going to another one as long as I live. It was horrible".

But he did though. And after nine years started the "We Agnostics" meeting. He was not a big fan of the Big Book, nor was he a fan of Chapter Four, according to Nick. "But he decided that he needed to call the meeting 'We Agnostics' so that there was some tie to Alcoholics Anonymous in general."

Shawn M describes "meeting hunting" in the Los Angeles AA directory when he came across the We Agnostics meeting and, curious, he decided to attend one of their meetings. He later wrote:

> *This was a group of people that did not subscribe to any notion of canned theology or cultish adherence to anything besides this: "no matter what" one does not put alcohol anywhere near the lips or nostrils. Also, if craving or life made you feel like jumping out of your skin, you must pick up the phone and talk with another meeting member. We help each other – "no matter what." That was the guiding principle of the LA We Agnostics AA group.*

At the end of the meeting, Charlie handed Shawn a piece of paper "that looked like one of the slips of paper from a fortune cookie" with the name "Charlie" on it along with a seven digit phone number.

This is what Charlie did. Over the course of more than four decades of sobriety, he had literally hundreds of sponsees. As his son put it, "He dedicated his life to helping others achieve sobriety, sponsoring hundreds to find a new way of living without alcohol."

He became Shawn's sponsor.

He was not an easy sponsor. Doing the Steps with Charlie was hardly a warm, pleasant experience. Brutal in fact. Much better than almost any shrink I had ever encountered and overwhelmingly wise. That was my first steps go around. Subsequent redoing of the Steps work proved simply enlightening with Charlie. It helped keep me sober then and still does now.

Charlie had had a tough life, which may in part explain why he was so devoted to helping others. His father had committed suicide when Charlie was 14 years old. His granddaughter, Angeliska, blamed this event for his alcoholism: "It was this tragedy that shaped who my grandfather would come to be: for half his life, an alcoholic who drowned his pain in drink, an actor, a collector of masks."

But he found AA. Angeliska (Angel) continues:

There is no doubt that this program saved his life, and my grandparent's marriage. Through AA my Grampa came through the tempest of his anger, his loss, and the void left by his father's death, to become one of the most serene and wise sages I have ever known.

Charlie was a staunch atheist. "His heritage was Jewish but unlike many atheistic Jews, Charlie did not observe the holidays or traditions. That would have been a treasonous act to Charlie," Shawn reports.

But he was a most spiritual man. Angel says: "My grandfather once told me that he was not a religious person, but that he was a spiritual person. I thank him for showing me, and many others, the freedom of that distinction." Shortly after his death, Angeliska posted her grandfather's favorite haiku online and it goes like this: "In the midst of a meadow / a skylark singing / free from everything". A number of people I talked to described him as one of the most spiritual human beings they had ever met.

Constantly being called upon to explain in AA his understanding of a "higher power," he eventually decided he could tolerate the notion that it was the "E" in "$E=MC^2$". It was "the total of all the energy in the universe," according to his granddaughter.

Charlie moved to Austin in 2000 to be closer to his sons. On August 21, 2001 he achieved another first by launching the "We Agnostics" group of Austin, Texas.

Shortly after that, on May 3, 2002, he helped Nick launch the Children of Chaos agnostic group. The group's name is based on a line from the second paragraph of Tradition Four, in the *Twelve and Twelve* book: "Children of chaos, we have defiantly played with every brand of fire…"

Charlie got things going in Austin.

"He was a big, important part of starting these meetings", Nick reported, "and he said that there were three things you could boil the steps down to: unconditional love, consistent responsibility and rigorous honesty".

When Charlie died in 2012 he was 98 years old and had more than 41 years of continuous sobriety. Hearing of his death, Shawn wrote:

> *Charlie gave unselfishly and saved countless lives. He did not care to keep score. He was a very devoted loving husband, father, grandfather and great-great-grandfather. Charlie was a significant contributor. He saved lives and reinstalled the ability to experience joy into many hearts. He was a holy man.*

He remained active in the program until the very end, holding AA meetings at his bedside and receiving AA visitors up to the last week of his life. Nick was there for his last chip in 2012.

Today, there are nine meetings for agnostics, atheists and freethinkers in Austin.

Intergroup for Austin – Hill County, it's called – also lists "Atheist / Agnostic" as a "meeting type". So if someone is looking for a meeting for atheists and agnostics in Austin there is a category called "Atheists / Agnostics" that can be clicked on.

By the way, the meeting that Charlie started in Hollywood in 1980 still meets every Tuesday and it's going strong.

Agnostic AA flourished in California in ways that it didn't flourish in other areas.

New York City and Boca Raton

The very first agnostic group in New York City was called "We Atheists" and its first meeting was held on September 10, 1986.

The group had three founders. They were Ada Halbeirch, David L and John Yablon. How they came together to do this is a remarkable story, all on its own.

The three – who did not know one another – answered an ad in the spring 1986 issue of *Free Inquiry*, a secular humanist magazine which, to this day, is circulated across America. The ad was from Harry, a Californian, and was addressed to atheist and agnostic members of AA who were having trouble with the religious nature of most meetings.

Over the next several weeks, Harry wrote to the three Easterners and provided encouragement and reassurance that they were not alone as agnostics trying to work the AA program to the best of their ability. He told them how it worked in Los Angeles and sent them a copy of the materials read at the agnostic group meeting he was involved with, We Agnostics of Pasadena.

Ada made the necessary arrangements with AA offices in New York and offered her apartment, on the upper east side of Manhattan, as a meeting site.

Ada was a very passionate woman, a socialist and a very wealthy New Yorker (her foundation continues to give to charities across the U.S.). She put together a meeting script, which is still used by the group today. It contains an extensive excerpt from Dr Bob's last talk, delivered at the First International AA Conference on July 30th, 1950, in Cleveland. In Ada's script, the meetings end with the group standing in a circle, holding hands, and chanting: "Live and let live".

Regular meetings of the We Agnostics of New York City AA group were soon in full swing with John Y and David L in attendance. Later the ever-growing group moved to its present location at the Jan Hus Church, where it still meets. The church found the word "Atheist" a bit harsh, and so the name of the group was changed to "We Humanists".

Much of the history in the preceding paragraphs is excerpted from the group's 1989 newsletter, called *Sampler*. The article was called, "Now It Can Be Told: A Bi-Coastal Tale of Two Cities." It was of course all about the tale of a city on the Pacific Coast, Los Angeles, and how someone from that city had come to the aid of alcoholics in New York City, on the Atlantic Coast.

After Ada helped to start the NYC meetings, she, a "snowbird from New York", was part of starting a We Agnostics meeting in 1987 in

Delray Beach, Florida. It was held at Crossroads, a large AA meeting hall, in a small non-smoking room across from the main room where traditional AA held its meetings. The other person involved was Henry Hellmuth, a native Floridian.

Henry always identified himself as Henry Half Measure. He believed that a lack of faith in gods was seen by AA as a half measure. He was very proud that this half measure availed him plenty of long term sobriety.

As soon as the Crossroads clubhouse realized that the meeting rejected God, however, they were at odds with each other and didn't get along. The We Agnostics group was getting kicked out of the Crossroads so in 1988 Ada and Henry moved the meeting to a Unitarian Fellowship church in Boca Raton. It still meets there to this day on Friday nights.

Two current members of the group, Valerie and Elizabeth, put together a brief history of the We Agnostics meeting in Boca Raton which, apparently, "went light on sponsorship and heavy on socialization". They add:

> *The focus (of the meeting) is on the sense of self identity and non religious openness to positive change – which some refer to as spiritual growth – connecting with others to share strengths and weaknesses. Alternative 12 Steps and Living Sober literature are read and are available today. It is common for the chair to read from "Language of the Heart", a piece which describes the practice of allowing all who enter to partake regardless of their religious affiliations or lack thereof. This alternative group is fiercely dedicated to keeping a non-didactic meeting open to provide a respite for those who do not attend traditional meetings. We Agnostics strive not only to remain sober but to enjoy the journey.*

Henry Hellmuth's sobriety date was August 16, 1982. He died Nov 6, 2014, with 32 years of sobriety.

Ada Halbeirch died in August, 2005, at the age of 83. She had more than 30 years of sobriety. Joan F, a member of We Humanists of New York City, visited Ada's grave site. She reported that, at Ada's request, her tombstone states that Ada "started an Alcoholics Anonymous meeting for Atheists and Agnostics".

John Yablon died on March 10, 2003. He was a co-founder of the Secular Humanist Society of New York City, a life-long resident of the Bronx and a veteran of World War II. Born in 1921, he got sober in 1962.

He was the kind of guy who makes a point of shaking hands with everyone in the room prior to an AA meeting. In November, 2002, John celebrated his 40th anniversary of sobriety and told those present, "I never said a prayer in my life".

David L, who now lives in Texas, got sober in 1980. He remembers as a child trying to figure out what people meant when they talked about God. "It didn't make any sense to me and I just couldn't do it. That lasted the rest of my life, pretty much." He said that when he got to AA, he had to "hang on to everything else," except the God part, to make it work.

Today, there are seventeen meetings in New York City for agnostics, atheists and freethinkers in AA. Under the search again for meetings there is something called a "special interest" category where you can click on "Agnostic" and again find these meetings.

[1] **A Different Road: Quad A Offers Help to Alcoholics Who Don't Buy Into God**: http://aaagnostica.org/2016/03/01/a-different-road/

Chapter 5:
More Rejection

Service, not Governance

One of the co-founders of AA, Bill Wilson, wrote this in the July, 1946, Grapevine:

> *So long as there is the slightest interest in sobriety, the most unmoral, the most anti-social, the most critical alcoholic may gather about him a few kindred spirits and announce to us that a new Alcoholics Anonymous Group has been formed. Anti-God, anti-medicine, anti-our Recovery Program, even anti-each other — these rampant individuals are still an AA Group if they think so!*

This quote does one thing and it does it very well. It explains Tradition Nine: "AA as such ought never be organized; but we may create **service** boards or committees directly responsible to those they **serve**". [Emphasis added.] Interestingly, the first version of the Traditions – at the time called "Twelve Points to Assure Our Future" – were written by Bill and published in the Grapevine a few months before the quote shared above, in April 1946.

So the original intent of this Tradition was quite clear: any AA organization has but one purpose: service. Not governance.

But some AA boards and committees don't understand. You can find them in Northern California, in Colorado, in Toronto and Vancouver, Canada.

Well, you can find them just about anywhere.

In an article published in the Grapevine in October 2016, life-j describes these AA organizations as our new "governing" bodies.

Indianapolis We Agnostics Group

Beyond Belief and We Agnostics in Toronto were not the first agnostic groups to be de-listed by an area Intergroup.

That dubious honour goes to the Indianapolis We Agnostics group. Founded on November 1, 2009, by Joe S, Heather B and Chris W, the group is the first and only agnostic group in Indiana.

And it wasn't just booted out once, but twice.

In a letter dated November 3, 2010, coincidentally on the group's first anniversary, signed by both the Indianapolis Intergroup office manager and the chairman, the members of We Agnostics were told that "your group reads a changed version of the Twelve Steps" and "It is the judgement of the Indianapolis Intergroup's Service Committee that your group has decided it is not an AA group".

It was quite a surprise to the group that they had made such a decision.

The authors of the letter go on to explain the reason for their de-listing. "Early in the Big Book our founders made it clear that we alcoholics suffer from a disease which only a spiritual experience can conquer."

Several group members met with the Indy Intergroup and We Agnostics was re-listed. They agreed that an adapted version of the 12 Steps would not be read at their meetings. In fact the We Agnostics "group conscience" was that literature that was not "Conference-approved" would not be included in the meeting format.

Nevertheless, the group was officially booted out a second time on May 8, 2011. This time no reason was given. Group members were not contacted. They were not told in advance that the issue was on the Intergroup agenda. They were not told of the allegations against them. They were not provided with an opportunity to offer any kind of defence. They were not even informed of the decision by Intergroup to de-list them but learned of it afterwards from a third party, accidentally.

It was kind of a hit and run incident.

An article in the July issue of the Indianapolis Intergroup, Inc. newsletter, The Paper, boasted that "Indy AA remains undiluted" as a consequence of the expulsion of We Agnostics.

"Nothing in the committee's decision in any way attempts to exclude or limit ANYONE from AA membership, so long as he/she has the requisite desire to stop drinking" the article goes on to say, suggesting that it's not acceptable to exclude an individual but it's okay to boot *groups* of nonbelievers – such as We Agnostics – out of AA.

One nonbeliever, no. Two or more, yes.

But is that true?

The Indy Intergroup clearly made an effort to present both sides of the debate around the de-listing of this group, or perhaps even any group. In the August issue of The Paper there is a lengthy article entitled, "The Other Side of the Story – Expelling a Local Group". In that article Donna H takes great exception with the expulsion of We Agnostics: "Simply, the Service Committee has greatly over-reached its boundaries (they are trusted servants, they do not govern) and have completely ignored at least six of our Traditions".

She goes on to say:

> *There was neither respect nor careful consideration; neither trust nor love. Personalities were everywhere and sadly not one Service Committee member asked themselves if there "might be another way to deal with this" or "maybe we should consult the traditions" or even "let's decide not to decide tonight". Instead there was a pound on the table, the decision made (not voted on mind you) and the meeting was ended.*

In some detail she then explains how Intergroup's actions violated six of the Traditions of AA.

The issue simmered and festered over the summer and into the fall.

And it did a lot of damage within the AA community in Indianapolis.

Virginia R, the AA area delegate for southern Indiana reported: "The committee's action caused all sorts of collateral damage. Long-time friendships were affected and there was a general sense of simmering hostility from all corners of our local AA community".

Faced with an unprecedented backlash, the Intergroup Service Committee met again on Thursday, October 6, and voted to re-list We Agnostics.

At this point, "it got very twisted", according to Joe S, a founder of We Agnostics, as he described the process of re-listing his group.

The de facto lawyer for the Service Group and the author of the article "Indy AA remains undiluted" in the July issue of the Indianapolis Intergroup newsletter, Stephen U, argued on Saturday, October 8, that the vote to re-list We Agnostics was "null and void".

Something to do with proper notice of the vote not having been provided.

A day later, on Sunday, October 9, a general membership meeting of the Indianapolis Intergroup was held.

At that meeting representatives of AA groups in Indianapolis expressed their lack of confidence in the Service Committee and voted ("something like 112-72", according to Donna) against the decision to de-list We Agnostics.

The following Thursday, October 13, 2011, the Service Committee met in a special meeting and voted, for a second time, to re-list We Agnostics.

Proper notice must have been provided this time, because the very next day – more than six months after having been de-listed – We Agnostics was back on the meeting list on Intergroup's website.

It was a gruelling experience for all involved.

At the time, Joe, who is the first to acknowledge that his own behaviour was not always impeccable, said that he was exhausted as a result of the controversy.

The area delegate, Virginia, reported that, "The whole ordeal was physically, emotionally and mentally exhausting. Glad to be done with it."

And the final outcome?

According to Joe, the Service Committee took the position that "if anyone complains about a meeting, they will be told to go to another meeting."

Des Moines Broad Highway Group

Let us not ignore the groups that aren't granted the opportunity to be booted off a regional list of AA meetings because, well, they aren't listed in the first place.

In Des Moines, Iowa, an agnostic group called The Broad Highway was founded on October 12, 2010.

Although the founders of the group registered it with the GSO, the Des Moines Intergroup refused to include the group in the meeting list.

On a Facebook page, the dilemma of the group was described rather sadly and ironically: "Your application to the Outcasts Club has been denied".

Don S and Tom H are the two founders of the group. Don – whose sobriety date goes back to June 14, 1991 – had 19 years of sobriety under his belt before he started The Broad Highway. He was a traditional member of AA for ten years before he "completely lost faith."

"Then, for about two years, I was nervous about my sobriety because of the God indoctrination I had received."

In most cities in North America, and in virtually all towns and villages, AA meetings end with people standing, holding hands, and reciting the Lord's Prayer.

Don ultimately decided he couldn't – and shouldn't – do that. He chose to remain seated during the closing prayer in order "to let others know that they are not alone and so that nonbelievers will feel welcome".

And that approach has been very helpful.

Don met the other founder of The Broad Highway Group at an "old school" AA meeting. He shared his lack of faith and Tom – who at the time had 23 years of sobriety – talked about his own doubt. The two had a long conversation after the meeting. Don reported that "when I started the agnostic meeting, Tom was always there. He often opened up and made the coffee. We would not have met if we were silent about our unbelief."

And Don met a sponsee in this way. "I sponsored one guy because he saw that I didn't participate in the prayer. He was returning to AA and was wary because he was now an atheist. He was tremendously relieved that there is a way to do AA without God."

When Don originally asked for the group's meetings to be listed on the Des Moines Intergroup meeting list, he was told that there was a six month waiting period. After six months he wrote and was told that the application was being referred to a committee.

Eventually Intergroup sent Jayson J to monitor a meeting of the Broad Highway. Don reports that the following exchange took place. Don told him that the group was registered with the GSO.

Jayson: "Well Intergroup won't take just anyone. There's more to it than that."

Don: "Then how can we meet your criteria?"

Jayson: "I don't know."

However, after six years, on November 13, 2016, the group was finally included in the Intergroup list. Don credited this, in part, to an article published in the Des Moines Register on February 5, 2015. The article was called "AA won't list nonreligious group meetings" and was critical of the local Intergroup. The author, Rekha Basu, correctly observed "This is an issue (AA) will need to grapple with to stay relevant. If the founders' goal was indeed not to promote any denomination, but to help people stay sober by sharing, surely there's room enough under the umbrella for all kinds – even godless people – to have a group".

Denver Freethinkers in AA Group

The first secular meeting of Freethinkers in AA in Denver, Colorado was held on October 2, 2013, with eight people in attendance. Two weeks later, there were 12 members, several of whom had stopped attending the religious meetings years ago.

After several months of the meetings attracting 15 to 20 members, it became clear that the group needed to expand to weekly meetings and to consider adding a second meeting. So, in July 2014, the Free-thinkers in AA Group became a weekly Monday 6:30 PM meeting and a Saturday 9:30 AM meeting.

The group – its listing never yet having been approved – again contacted the Denver Central Office Manager to request a print and online listing of these group meetings, which were duly registered with the General Service Office in New York. The manager flatly refused the listing, saying "We wouldn't want a newcomer to attend your meeting and think it is representative of what AA really is". She later sent out people to spy on the group and report back. The group apparently didn't meet her standards.

To add insult to injury, when she was sent the name of the group's Intergroup Representative, the Denver Central Office Manager responded that the Freethinkers in AA Group "cannot have represent-ation on the Central Office Committee" since it is "not a recognized group".

One of the main founders of the group, Jeb B, expressed his frustra-tion this way:

I find it incredibly unfortunate that 12-Step programs and treatment programs recommending them cannot let go of the religious origins and practices like prayer to an imaginary being. No one seeking recovery should be required to participate in religious practices, prayers, of any kind. Such programs are missing the boat by failing to utilize the proven cognitive-behavioral process constituting the true 12-Step program. Spiritual make-believe has no place in government programs of our constitutional secular society.

Freethinkers in AA continues to thrive, and has 140 men and women on its confidential group list. The group makes quarterly contributions to AA World Services and District 9 and Area 10 of AA. Its next outreach effort will be to contact all area treatment facilities with information about the group and its meetings.

Laytonville Freethinkers Group

It took three years after a meeting had been started for it to be listed. That happened in Laytonville, California, and it's a bit of complicated story.

In April 2013 life-j approached the Mendocino Inland Intergroup to get a meeting he and a few others were planning, the Laytonville Free-thinkers Group, listed in the local meeting directory. A couple of people objected and they rallied their forces against the group. The fight kept on until February 2014 when life-j finally gave up trying to have it included in the meeting list.

The group went ahead and held the first Laytonville Freethinkers meeting on August 22, 2013. It was one of five AA meetings in Layton-ville, which has a population of less than 1,500.

And it wouldn't be listed until October 2016.

It was in that month in 2016 that the AA Grapevine published an issue devoted to "Atheist and Agnostic Members" of AA. There were half a dozen articles in that issue written by atheists and one of the best was called Open-Minded.[1] It was written by life-j and in it he discussed his problem getting his meeting listed in "liberal Northern California".

Well, that article got read at meetings in Laytonville and at other meet-ings in the area and the next time the Mendocino Inland Intergroup met it was decided to include the Laytonville Freethinkers meeting in the meeting directory.

It took three years for a modicum of acceptance to finally be realized and acted upon.

Go figure.

Vancouver We Agnostics and Sober Agnostics Groups

It is not just in Toronto where things got ugly in AA and groups got booted out.

It happened in Vancouver too.

One of the key players in starting agnostic meetings in Vancouver was a fellow by the name of Denis Kilborn. His sobriety date was April 28, 1975 and he died from cancer complications on April 1, 2016. As Dan V put it, "In his 41 years in AA he helped countless numbers of people, as a sponsor and as a friend. AA was his life... Denis was not only my sponsor for 32 years but also my trusted friend."

Oddly enough, after some 25 years sober in AA Denis realized he had a problem and checked himself into treatment centre.

How many people do you know who do that? And what was the problem? Dan reports:

> It had everything to do with his belief system. He had faked it for so long in AA and could no longer handle the internal struggles as a result. "What do I believe? What don't I believe?" were the questions on the table in that period of treatment. And that's where he started verbalizing his lack of belief in God.
>
> Now he had this new-found idea that you actually can get sober and maintain sobriety at a level that is conducive to a good life without a God. Well, this is going against everything that he had heard over the last twenty-five years! His big question then was, "Who do I share that with?" It was then that a decision was made to help widen the path of AA for all who suffer.
>
> Denis started the first agnostic AA meeting in the city of Vancouver.

Denis chose to do that, as he put, rather than "si
dogma and the rituals that had taken over many of the
Things like ending the meetings by holding hands and
calls out 'Who's the boss?' and everyone recites the Lor

A woman
gender
to'

It was a men's meeting called "We Agnostics" and
Monday nights. The meeting was duly registered with b ...ie New
York GSO and the Greater Vancouver Intergroup Society in the
summer of 2012.

A year later Denis helped start another meeting, this one called
"Sober Agnostics". Its founding meeting was held on May 7, 2013 and
the meeting is still going strong today. Indeed, an updated "How It
Works", put together by one of its members Hilary J and adopted by
the group, can be found in **Appendix I: Secular Versions of "How It
Works"**.

This meeting too was registered with the General Service Office in
New York and with the Vancouver Intergroup.

However, problems were on their way. As Hilary reports:

> *Our meeting soon attracted the attention of the
> Vancouver Intergroup operating committee. The
> committee chair, Jim J., attended incognito to "see what
> we were up to", announcing himself at the end of the
> meeting. When the next edition of the directory was
> published, Sober Agnostics had been deleted.*

> *This precipitated lengthy, sometimes hostile debates at
> the monthly Intergroup meetings.*

> *Since we had changed the Steps, and did not use the
> official AA literature, were we really an AA group? Did
> the operating committee have the authority to decide
> whether we should be listed? A package was issued to
> all Intergroup reps to take back to their home groups for
> group conscience. After months of agonizing debate
> and delays, the final vote was on whether Intergroup
> should continue to discuss the matter. The verdict was
> "No", and that was the end of that.*

That verdict took place on Tuesday, January 21, 2014.

, almost in tears, said she could not understand how the vote
the way it did in view of Tradition Three and AA's commitment
be inclusive rather than exclusive.

But it was over and the issue decided. Members of the banned
agnostic groups had never been given the opportunity to defend their
rights within AA and the matter was closed.

"Every group has the right to be wrong," Bill Wilson once wrote. (12
and 12, p. 47)

And the Greater Vancouver Intergroup Society (GVIS) exercised that
right.

The problem wouldn't be resolved for almost four years. The last time
the agnostic groups had been listed in the GVIS meeting directory
was in June of 2013.

In 2017 it was finally decided to reopen the issue and to have an
actual vote on whether or not these groups should be listed and not
leave that decision solely to the Intergroup operating committee. The
vote took place on March 21, 2017. There were some 50 people
present and there was a long and difficult discussion. A two-thirds
majority – 31 votes – was required in order to list the secular groups
and re-admit them as voting members of the Greater Vancouver Intergroup Society.

The result?

Thirty-three people voted to "list all groups that wish to be listed".

One Alcoholic Judging Another

> *The way our "worthy" alcoholics have sometimes tried
> to judge the "less worthy" is, as we look back on it,
> rather comical. Imagine, if you can, one alcoholic
> judging another!*

> *Bill W.*

It is important to note that these are not the only agnostic groups that
have been brutalized or intimidated within traditional AA.

It happens all the time and everywhere, around the world.

For example, I went to my AA Central Office a few days ago to put
flyers on the shelves, announcing the first anniversary of our "We
Agnostics" group in Hamilton. There are many flyers there, announ-

cing new groups, birthdays, the cancellation of meetings, and the like. The volunteer working in the office looked at the flyers and said, "You can't put those up". We argued about it and she ended up phoning the manager, Jimmy, who said it was all right to share them. The problem for her, of course, was the name of the group: We Agnostics.

Can we imagine "one alcoholic judging another"? Sure we can.

Just ask the alcoholic that doesn't buy the "God bit" whether or not she has been judged in the rooms of Alcoholics Anonymous.

[1] **Open-Minded**: http://aaagnostica.org/2016/09/22/open-minded/

Chapter 6:
Changing the 12 Steps

As time passes our book literature has a tendency to get more and more frozen – a tendency for conversion into something like dogma. This is a trait of human nature which I am afraid we can do little about.

Bill Wilson, Correspondence, 1961

Much of the controversy with regard to secular groups has to do with changing the 12 Steps of AA.

This has been particularly true since two agnostic groups were booted out of the Greater Toronto Area Intergroup for posting a secular version of the Steps online.

But it is not just a problem in Toronto.

And it has not only been a problem with Intergroups in various locations across North America, but it has also plagued the General Service Office.

One example. On September 28, 2010, Gayle S R, a GSO staffer, wrote to the administrator of the Agnostic AA NYC website. In the letter Gayle points out that the website refers to "addicts" as well as alcoholics – a no-no in "old school" AA. Worse, a secular version of the 12 Steps was available on the website.

"So we respectfully request that your group stop calling itself an AA group," Gayle concluded. The modified 12 Steps, and any reference to addicts, were removed from the website.

You can't change the Steps, some will argue. If you do, you are not AA.

After all, the Steps are copyrighted and the copyright is owned by AA World Services.

Moreover, in 1957 the following bylaw was adopted by AA "the General Service Board asserts the negative right of preventing, so far as it may be within its power so to do, any modification, alteration, or extension of these Twelve Steps, except at the instance of the Fellowship of Alcoholics Anonymous in keeping with the Charter of the General Service Conference".

In keeping with the Charter, it would apparently require a two-thirds vote to amend the Steps.

So, isn't it pretty obvious that a person or group who rewrites the Steps should be booted out of AA, as was done to the two groups here in Toronto?

In spite of the quote about the "General Service Board asserts the negative right", the answer is "absolutely not".

Nobody is trying to change the AA Steps, as originally published in 1939.

However, groups and individuals have a right to their own version. These adapted versions are not meant to replace the original 12 Steps, but are solely for the use of the group, based upon the conscience of its members, or the individual and her or his conscience and beliefs (or lack thereof).

And the author of the Steps, Bill Wilson, was comfortable with that. He was very, very comfortable with adaptations of the 12 Steps within AA.

When told that some Buddhists wanted to start AA groups in Thailand but wished to change the word "God" in the Steps to "good", Bill wrote:

> *To some of us, the idea of substituting "good" for "God" in the Twelve Steps will seem like a watering down of AA's message. We must remember that AA's Steps are suggestions only. A belief in them as they stand is not at all a requirement for membership among us. This liberty has made AA available to thousands who never would have tried at all, had we insisted on the Twelve Steps just as written. (Alcoholics Anonymous Comes of Age, Page 81, 1957)*

Let's further explore three points mentioned in Bill's remarks.

First, "AA's Steps are suggestions only". It says so right on page 59 of the Big Book. The Steps as "suggestions" are copyrighted! Atheists and agnostics like Jim Burwell lobbied hard back in 1939 for this and other changes and Bill appreciated these contributions, crediting them with "widening the gateway" of the fellowship.

So there is a very serious problem when the Greater Toronto Area Intergroup (GTAI) says "a group must be prepared to practice the 12 steps". (More shall be revealed about the position of the GTAI in the next chapter.)

You don't boot someone out for not following a suggestion. That is wrong. That is a form of fanaticism, authoritarianism.

Second, "A belief in them as they stand is not at all a requirement for membership among us".

"As they stand" is an idiom that means "as they are now" or "as they exist at present". So you don't have to believe in the Steps ("them") as they are now, as they stand, in order to be a member of Alcoholics Anonymous.

And yet agnostic groups in various towns and cities in North America have been excluded from or booted out of the fellowship simply because they do not believe in the Steps "as they stand".

Amazing. Truly amazing.

How many times in AA literature do we have to be told that "the only requirement for AA membership is a desire to stop drinking"? How many times do we have to be told that membership does not depend upon "conformity"? How many times do we have to hear that "each alcoholic among us is a member of AA, so long as he or she so declares"?

Third, AA is available to more people – atheists and agnostics, in particular – because the fellowship does not insist upon the Twelve Steps "just as written".

Think about it a bit.

If God can be "as we understand Him" then surely – surely to god, so to speak – we can interpret the Steps as we wish.

That should be obvious to anyone.

It could even be argued that an individual interpretation of the Steps is not only unavoidable but it is, in the end, essential.

For those who use the Steps as a tool in recovery – and let's be clear, not everyone in AA does that and it is not a requirement for membership – this quote from two women who wrote their own interpretation of the Steps in 1991 is very relevant: "We can learn the universal, generic pattern of life's dance from the 12 Steps. But in our individual dance of life, we choose our own music and dance our own dance".

An atheist or agnostic can't really be expected to accept Steps in which "God", "Him" or "Power" (with a capital P) are mentioned six times. To thine own self be true.

"To thine own self be true" is important to many of us in recovery and in AA. So what to do? The agnostic can't come to your meeting? She can't start her own group?

Those who insist on the Steps as they were dictated in 1939 often come across as, well, dictators. And that's certainly how the GTA Intergroup behaved when it put the boots to the two agnostic groups in Toronto.

At least three reasons have been listed as to why individuals and groups should not be excluded from the fellowship of AA for putting together their own versions of the 12 Steps.

But it's worth repeating: Nobody is trying to change the original AA Steps, as published in 1939. Adapted versions are not meant to replace the original 12 Steps, but are solely for the use of the group, based upon the conscience of its members, or the individual and her or his conscience and beliefs (or lack thereof).

It all has to do with the very nature of AA.

There are no requirements in AA. There are no "musts". As Bill once put it, talking about Tradition Three, "That means that these two or three alcoholics could try for sobriety in any way they liked. They could disagree with any or all of AA's principles and still call themselves an AA group".

That can be hard for some people to accept.

But all of this means – the very nature of our fellowship requires – that we quit putting the boots to women and men who have created their own personal interpretations of the 12 Steps based upon an honest individual or group conscience.

The Greater Toronto Area Intergroup got it wrong. And it's up to the rest of us, including AA World Services, to put things back together and invite "anyone anywhere" with a desire to stop drinking to join together with all of us underneath the AA umbrella.

We need their support. They need our support. This is AA.

Chapter 7:
Agnostics and Human Rights

Let's begin by looking at some dates of historical significance.

May 31, 2011. Two agnostic AA groups, Beyond Belief and We Agnostics, are voted out of the Greater Toronto Area Intergroup (GTAI) and off of the area AA meeting lists. The motion to de-list the groups was carried by a vote of 24 to 15, with 9 abstentions.

March 27, 2012. A motion to re-list the two groups was defeated by a vote of 59 to 19. The actual motion read as follows: "that the two groups, Beyond Belief and We Agnostics, be re-listed in the Meeting Book and reinstated as members of Toronto Intergroup".

April 24, 2012. The group *Widening Our Gateway*, which had been a member of the Greater Toronto Area (GTA) Intergroup since its first meeting on October 16, 2011, was officially "suspended from any involvement at Toronto Intergroup" by a vote of 27 to 17.

September 18, 2014. A formal application alleging discrimination against the groups based on creed is filed with the Human Rights Tribunal of Ontario by Larry K.

October 2, 2015. The Tribunal issues its first Interim Decision which states that the three respondents to Larry's complaint are: The General Services Board of Alcoholics Anonymous Inc., AA World Services, Inc. and the Greater Toronto Area Intergroup. A request to remove AA World Services as a respondent was denied.

January 13, 2016. An Ontario Human Rights Tribunal summary hearing is held between the applicant and the respondents.

February 17, 2016. The Tribunal releases its second Interim Decision (see below).

May 2016. Both the complainant and the GTAI filed their responses to the Interim Decision. Nothing has changed, really, from the Interim Decision. The matter will be resolved either through mediation or in a Court Decision.

November 18, 2016. First mediation session. The Tribunal asks every person who files a human rights application and every person or organization responding to the application to participate in mediation in order to attempt to reach a settlement, that is, to resolve the issues raised in the application without going to a formal hearing.

January 18, 2017. Second mediation session. If the issue is not resolved in the first session, a second mediation session can be held.

January 31, 2017. At the monthly meeting of the GTAI, the chair announces that a resolution has been reached and the ousted groups are to be re-listed. And, once again, after almost six years, secular groups shall be legitimate and respected members of the Greater Toronto Area Intergroup.

The expulsion of the agnostic groups took place in 2011 and 2012.

It should be noted that the General Service Office (GSO), based in New York, was certainly not oblivious to what was going on north of the border and, indeed, played a role in the de-listing of Beyond Belief and We Agnostics.

Asked if a group can adapt the Steps, a GSO staffer, Mary Clare L wrote: "If we are aware that an AA Group listed here at GSO has in any way modified the AA Steps we do not list them". This is from an email on April 4, 2011, and is reported in the July issue of the GTA Intergroup's newsletter "Better Times".

But Mary Clare realized that she had made a mistake, and, to her credit, in a letter to the GSO area delegate, Robb W, on June 14, she wrote: "I need to correct a misstatement on the text that I sent you because my understanding of what happens here at GSO was wrong". She continued:

> As embodied in the Fourth Tradition, the formation and operation of an AA Group resides within the group conscience of its members… Groups listed in the directory are listed at their own request… It is not any AA member or AA group's right to stand in judgment of another.

Mary Clare offered to "make amends" by sending her correction to groups in the area.

And to the credit of the GTA Intergroup, Mary Clare's correction is printed in an "apology" in the September issue of "Better Times".

But the damage had already been done. The groups were out.

When it came to de-listing the third group, Widening Our Gateway, the Intergroup executive shared a letter from Robb W, the Area 86 delegate to the General Service Conference. Even though it might well be argued that it was Robb's job to be aware of the viewpoints of all AA members in his region and represent those views at General Service Conferences, and even though Robb had repeatedly been invited to attend a meeting of either Beyond Belief or We Agnostics, he had never bothered to do so, or in any other way become aware of the "experience, strength and hope" of these women and men, all duly recognized as members of AA by the organization for which he toiled, the General Service Office. Nevertheless, it was his opinion that agnostic groups should "not imply affiliation with Alcoholics Anonymous" as they share an adapted version of the 12 steps.

We do not ask anyone to believe anything when they arrive at the doors of AA, he wrote. However, "It is hoped that people will 'come to believe' as I did through working the 12 Steps of AA".

According to Robb's thinking, if you don't come to believe, or are not at least prepared to come to believe, then you are simply not real AA.

One of the founders of We Agnostics, Larry K, tirelessly challenged the Intergroup decision to boot his group out of the GTA Intergroup and off of the regional AA meeting lists.

He wrote letters. He talked to members of the Intergroup Executive. He raised the issue with AA World Services. Sometimes it looked like there was reason for hope. Sometimes not.

This went on for two years.

Finally, on September 18, 2014 Larry lodged a complaint with the Human Rights Tribunal of Ontario.

Why? Because we humans, no matter what organization we do or do not belong to, are required to abide by laws guaranteeing equality and prohibiting discrimination.

In Ontario, a Human Rights Code took effect in 1962, and was the first Human Rights Code of its kind in Canada. It provides that every person has a right to equal treatment with respect to services, goods, and facilities without discrimination because of creed (including atheism and agnosticism). One of the things that the Ontario Human Rights Commission says is this:

> *It is the OHRC's position that every person has the right to be free from discriminatory or harassing behaviour*

that is based on religion or which arises because the person who is the target of the behaviour does not share the same faith. This principle extends to situations where the person who is the target of such behaviour has no religious beliefs whatsoever, including atheists and agnostics who may, in these circumstances, benefit from the protection set out in the Code.

Larry K's argument was very simple: If AA is for everyone, if it is not religious, then it was a violation of the Human Rights Code to exclude his AA group.

The groups had been booted out because they changed the Steps. The "suggested" program of AA, the 12 Steps, has the word "God", "Him" or "Power" in them six times. Obviously that is not going to work for an agnostic or atheist. Interpreting the Steps without God is pretty much inevitable for an atheist and his or her group.

But if AA is "spiritual and not religious" and if the only requirement for membership is "a desire to stop drinking" can agnostic groups really be booted out? Even if they adapt the "suggested" 12 Steps to their own understanding and needs?

A very good question.

There were two hearings on the subject. In the first hearing – Interim Decision October 2015 – the General Service Board and AA World Services attempted to distance themselves from Intergroup – they had, after all, not expelled the two groups – and thus be removed as respondents at the Human Rights Tribunal. The Vice-Chairperson said no: all of the literature upon which the GTA Intergroup had based its behavior and decisions was owned, copyrighted, distributed and promoted by the General Service Board and AA World Services. They thus shared legal culpability for the expulsion of the two secular groups.

What follows are the relevant points 2, 7, 8, 9 and (part of) 10 of the second interim decision of the Human Rights Tribunal released on February 17, 2016 and based upon the second hearing which had been held in January.

———

[2] The applicant alleges, among other things, that the respondent, GTA Intergroup of Alcoholics Anonymous (GTAI), is responsible for

48

maintaining a list of all Alcoholics Anonymous meetings in the Greater Toronto Area. The applicant alleges that GTAI removed the applicant's Alcoholics Anonymous group from its directory, website listing and listing given over the phone because the group members are agnostic. It is further alleged that the members of the applicant's group have been denied the right to vote and to have their voices heard on matters that are important to all AA members...

[7] The respondent, GTAI, submits that the Alcoholics Anonymous (AA) recovery program follows 12 steps and that these steps involve a belief in God. GTAI submits that evidence indicates that its purpose is to practice the 12 steps and practice a belief in God. In order to be part of GTAI, a group must be prepared to practice the 12 steps and thus the members of the group must have a belief in God. GTAI submits that it is not denying the applicant's group the right to form its own intergroup and follow its own process.

[8] GTAI submits that it is a special interest group that is protected, by section 18 of the Code, from a finding that it has breached the applicant's Code rights. Section 18 of the Code states,

> *Rights ... are not infringed where membership or participation in a religious, philanthropic, educational, fraternal or social institution or organization that is primarily engaged in serving the interests of persons identified by a prohibited ground of discrimination is restricted to persons who are similarly identified.*

[9] GTAI also submits that it is a bona fide requirement that groups that wish to be part of this intergroup must have a belief in the higher power of God.

[10] The applicant submits that AA is a fellowship of men and women who share the common desire to achieve sobriety. The only requirement for membership in AA is this desire to achieve sobriety and to help others in this achievement...

———

Obviously based upon points 7 through 9 above, the Greater Toronto Area Intergroup believes that a belief in God is a necessary part of being a part of its organization. And as expressed in point 8, it seeks to rely on an exception in the Code which allows "religious organizations" to exclude those who are not like-minded from membership or participation, in this case atheists and agnostics.

49

The only way an organization can legitimately ban nonbelievers, according to the Human Rights Code, is if, well, it is a religious organization. That is permitted by Section 18 of the Code where an organization identifies itself as a "special interest organization". In this case, a religious organization.

This is, to put it mildly, an unusual view within Alcoholics Anonymous.

And this position of the GTAI was not well received by AA World Services and the AA General Services Board.

In fact, the General Service Board, at its quarterly meeting on October 31, 2016 essentially decided to kick the GTAI out of AA. This was reported in the Quarterly Report from the GSO (page 5):

> *A motion was made that AAWS, Inc. remove all database directory listings of the Greater Toronto Area Intergroup based on their response to the Ontario Human Rights Tribunal that they are a religious organization. The motion was adopted unanimously by the AAWS Board.*

The GSO's decision to "de-list" the Greater Toronto Area Intergroup came just before two mediation sessions between Larry and the GTAI, held on November 18, 2016 and January 18, 2017. The Tribunal asks every person who files a human rights application (the Applicant) and every person or organization responding to a human rights application (the Respondent(s)) to participate in mediation in order to attempt to reach a settlement, that is, to resolve the issues raised in the application without going to a formal hearing.

And it was in these mediation sessions that the GTAI yielded to the GSO.

And yielded to agnostics in AA.

The GTAI released a report, and a copy of the settlement, at its monthly meeting on January 31, 2017.

In the report, the Greater Toronto Area Intergroup does a complete about-face and writes: "GTA Intergroup acknowledges that the manner in which individual AA members or groups of AA members interpret and apply the Steps and Traditions in their own lives is a matter for those individuals alone."

And then in the settlement document, the crux of their concession is as follows:

It is acknowledged by the parties hereto that any AA group meeting as an autonomous group without any other affiliation and acknowledging or adopting the suggested AA Twelve Steps for the individual and the Twelve Traditions of AA for the group can be recognized as a participating group in the GTA Intergroup and, for greater clarity, this is regardless of the specific beliefs or practices of the group members or the group as a whole.

This is very interesting. And to see why, let's back up just a little bit.

Following the expulsion of the Widening Our Gateway group in April of 2012, the Port Credit Group moved that the GTA Intergroup Procedures and Guidelines be changed "to make it perfectly clear that an AA group needs to adopt the 12 Steps, 12 Traditions and 12 Concepts of AA."

And so a motion was put together and it said the following: "An AA group needs to adopt only the 12 Steps, 12 Traditions and 12 Concepts of AA, as adopted by the AA General Service Board, in order to be recognized as an AA group by GTA Intergroup". The motion was put to a so-called "referendum" and the results announced in June. The final tally was 832 for the motion, and 286 against. (Out of the 330 groups in the GTA at the time, only 72 voted and the tally reflects the number of members in each group present for the business meetings in which the vote was held.)

The motion does not include the word "acknowledge". It specifically requires the "adoption" of the 12 Steps, etc., by a group if it is to be a member of the GTAI.

"Acknowledgement" is not a major problem. It is not acceptance or adoption. It is simply recognizing how, for example, the 12 Steps were written in 1939. Nothing new here. The reading of the secular 12 Steps at Beyond Belief had always been preceded with the statement, "This version is adapted from the original 12 Steps which were first published in 1939 in Chapter 5 of Alcoholic Anonymous."

But it is very interesting that while there had initially been a referendum to order all groups wanting to be members of the GTAI to "adopt" the 12 Steps as originally written, the GTAI Ad Hoc Sub-Committee charged with resolving the Human Rights Tribunal complaint apparently felt no need to consult a single group or member to add the word "acknowledge" to that membership requirement.

51

But there you go. That's the GTA Intergroup. In a full concession to we agnostics in AA, and our rights within the fellowship, their report – using the "acknowledgment" principle again, but this time for itself – goes on to state:

> GTA Intergroup acknowledges that the manner in which individual AA members or groups of AA members interpret and apply the Steps and Traditions in their own lives is a matter for those individuals alone.

Those words – and the word "acknowledge" added to its Procedures and Guidelines motion – are the very essence of what the GTAI had to do to achieve a Human Rights Tribunal settlement.

Still, the GTAI failed to understand its own failings and the damage it had done to alcoholics and to the fellowship. One of the paragraphs in its report was particularly bizarre: "It has been, and remains, the GTAI's position that there has been no discrimination against the complainant, or indeed anyone else, let alone on the prohibited ground of creed".

What?

The GTAI booted groups out – Beyond Belief and We Agnostics on May 31, 2011 and Widening Our Gateway on April 24, 2012 – simply because the groups don't buy the idea that God is the source of their sobriety. That's not a form of discrimination against the complainant? Or anyone else? That's not discrimination based upon the prohibited ground of creed?

What is it then?

The GTAI did however concede that when Larry K first went to them to express his concerns, "the response to those concerns was not as constructive as it could have been".

No, really? It only took five years. And legal action. And a threat from the GSO.

It makes one wonder whether the GTAI understands Tradition Three. Or Steps 4, 5, 6, 7, 8, 9 and 10.

Maybe it should boot itself out. Of itself.

Ultimately, Intergroup had little choice but to yield to we agnostics in AA and put aside its religious dogmatism and recognize, if only reluctantly and certainly not wholeheartedly, that the way "individual AA members or groups of AA members interpret and apply the Steps and Traditions in their own lives is a matter for those individuals alone".

That is AA. Or AA as it was meant to be, before and after the behaviour that the GTAI displayed because a few had the gall to ignore its dogmatic "my way or the highway" approach to recovery in AA. "All people must necessarily rally to the call of their own particular convictions and we of AA are no exception." Bill Wilson said that. He was right.

Let us end this chapter with something that needs to be said.

Thank you Larry K!

We can only imagine what Larry went through over five years of expulsion and litigation. But he did the right thing. His work was without a doubt important for agnostics in AA. And it is crucial for AA.

If AA is to move forward.

Part Two:
Problems in AA

Chapter 8:
Accepting Special Composition Groups

Since the very beginning, there have been special composition groups in Alcoholics Anonymous.

And their acceptance, sadly, has always posed a problem. "'Special' groups have always been viewed with suspicion, alarm and sometimes outright hostility within AA." (**Special Composition Groups in AA**[1])

We nonbelievers are thus not alone when it comes to being treated as outsiders or outcasts.

We shall look at four of these special groupings, pretty much in the order in which they came to be recognized within the fellowship: Women, Blacks, Young People and the LGBTQ community.

Women

The first women in AA were not immediately well-received. When Dr. Bob was told that a woman, Sylvia K, was on her way to his AA meeting in Akron in the late summer of 1939, "Dr. Bob threw up his hands and said, 'We have NEVER had a woman and will NOT work on a woman.'" (*Dr. Bob and the Good Oldtimers*, p. 180)

As it turned out, Sylvia was the first woman to achieve long term sobriety in AA and her personal story, "The Keys of the Kingdom", appears in the 2nd, 3rd, and 4th editions of the Big Book.

Another early woman member of AA wrote an article in the AA Grapevine in June of 1960 called "For Men Only?" She reported attending her first AA meeting at "Bill and Lois's brownstone house" on April 11, 1939. She was the only woman alcoholic at that meeting. She reports that many of the older members treated her as a "freak" and the newer male members would sometimes say something like, "If there's one think I can't stand, it's to see a woman drunk!" While overall most of the men "fully accepted me as one of themselves… there remained a curious loneliness, nonetheless".

Acceptance of women in AA did not come quickly, nor was it universal.

As the author reports:

I thought the corner had been turned, that no one could ever again imagine AA was "for men only." Imagine my shock and horror when in December 1959, twenty years and eight months after my solo landing in AA, a woman member in a great midwestern city I was visiting told me of several AA groups in the city who would not receive women as members – stated flatly that they did not want women in their groups. Several men with us corroborated her story, adding, before I could catch my breath, that it didn't matter so much in a big city like theirs where there were plenty of other groups a woman could go to, but what bothered them was the fact that this was true in many small cities and towns where there was only one group, so that in effect this meant denying AA to women alcoholics.

The author of this article, named as "Anonymous" when it was published in the Grapevine in 1960, was actually Marty Mann.

Marty had her own problems with the Big Book. Early in that article, she writes: "This was a man's book, entirely about men, obviously written by and for men, and a particular kind of men at that – religious men".

In her biography "Women Suffer Too", also published in the 2nd, 3rd and 4th editions of the Big Book, it is also pretty clear that Marty was not a big fan of the "God bit" in AA. She writes, "I couldn't stomach religion, and I didn't like the mention of God or any of the other capital letters. If that was the way out it wasn't for me".

But clearly what worked was the fellowship, one alcoholic talking to another alcoholic:

I went trembling into a house in Brooklyn filled with strangers… and I found I had come home at last, to my own kind… I had found my salvation. I wasn't alone any more. That was the beginning of a new life, a fuller life, a happier life than I had ever known or believed possible. I had found friends, understanding friends… Talking things over with them, great floods of enlightenment showed me myself as I really was and I was like them.

Marty Mann would not only become one of the more important women in early AA, she became one of the more important people in early AA. Bill was her friend and sponsor, and one of the few people who knew that she was a lesbian.

With the encouragement of Bill Wilson, she founded the National Committee for Education on Alcoholism, Inc. (NCEA) – eventually renamed the National Council on Alcoholism – which first opened its doors on October 2, 1944. According to Bob K, its core message was:

1. Alcoholism is a disease, and the alcoholic is a sick person;

2. The alcoholic can be helped, and is worth helping;

3. Alcoholism is a public health problem, and therefore a public responsibility.

"These ideas are so universally accepted today, that it can be difficult to imagine that they were both revolutionary and counter-intuitive at the time." (**Key Players in AA History**[2])

Marty wrote two key books on alcoholism and played a major role in bringing about the "Hughes Act", the Comprehensive Alcohol Abuse and Alcoholism Prevention, Treatment, and Rehabilitation Act of 1970, which enhanced the federal government's role in alcoholism treatment and prevention and was a key part in shaping the understanding of alcoholism.

She made her last public appearance at the AA International Convention in 1980 in New Orleans. She was greeted with thunderous applause. Marty died just a few weeks later on July 22 at the age of 75.

Women's groups were, and a great deal of credit is owed to Marty Mann, the first "special composition" groups in AA, with the first group specifically for women launched in June, 1941 in Cleveland, Ohio.

In February of 1964 a first national conference for women in AA was held in Kansas City, Missouri. Forty-five women were present at the first conference and one has since been held annually ever since with attendance now in the hundreds. "The permanent motto of the event is, 'The Language of the Heart Will Be Spoken Here'". (Special Composition Groups in AA)

Black People

As is recorded in the Special Compositions Group document, "AA is inescapably a part of the society in which it exists. And when the Fellowship was founded – and for three decades thereafter – de facto discrimination against Blacks was accepted in many places".

Some of this discrimination is demonstrated in *Pass It On*, when Bill Wilson invited two Black alcoholics to the New York City meeting. A couple of AA members were outraged and "ready to secede from AA and walk out". After some discussion a "compromise method of permitting blacks to come to meetings as 'observers' worked" and became a model for Blacks at AA meetings. (**Pass It On**[3])

Deirdre S gave a rather wonderful talk at the Austin Convention in 2016 called **A History of Special Interest Groups in AA**[4]. She reported talking to a friend, Bob F, who "said that up into the 1970s de-facto segregation existed. As a Black member of AA you could go to any meeting, but you had to sit in the back and couldn't share unless it was a meeting that catered to Black members".

This is no doubt why Black members of AA formed their own groups early on. By 1945 there were Black groups in Washington, DC, and St. Louis, Missouri. ("Jim's Story", which appeared in the second and third editions of the Big Book, was written by "the originator of AA's first black group" in Washington.) In 1947, the first colored group began in Harlem. But still they were not well accommodated. Deirdre's friend Bob F reported that a letter had been sent to Intergroup in New York City in 1957 "asking if Black members could participate in the Intergroup delegates meeting".

It is generally acknowledged that "AA has never enjoyed a percentage of Black membership equivalent to the percentage of Blacks in the general population". (Special Composition Groups in AA)

Black meetings have never been and are not now a separate category in the AA Directories and in most Intergroup meeting lists. It is also worth noting that it was not until 2001 that the first "Conference-approved" pamphlet by and for Blacks, "*AA for the Black and African American Alcoholic*", originally called "*Can AA Help Me Too? African Americans Share Their Stories*", was published.

Sixty years to produce a "Conference-approved" pamphlet for Blacks and African Americans?

Young People

Meetings for young people – women and men under the age of 35 – began popping up in 1946. They were begun in Philadelphia, San Diego and New York City. "Young people's groups were often regarded with suspicion by older groups. Not uncommonly, they were not included in the local service structure because they were 'not AA'." (Special Composition Groups in AA)

But the movement continued to grow, with more and more meetings across North America. The first International Conference of Young People in Alcoholics Anonymous (ICYPAA) was held in Niagara Falls, New York, in April of 1958. "It was immediately accused of being some kind of non-affiliated splinter group... ICYPAA leaders kept insisting, 'We're not a separate movement or a breaking-away from Alcoholics Anonymous'." (Special Composition Groups in AA) Indeed, there is mutual support and respect between ICYPAA and the General Service Board of Alcoholics Anonymous.

LGBTQ

The LGBTQ community has been an important part of making AA more inclusive.

In fact, we owe these folks one of the most important traditions in the fellowship, Tradition Three: "The only requirement for membership is a desire to stop drinking".

In 1937, an alcoholic approached one of AA's co-founders and said, "Dr. Bob, I've got a real problem to pose to you. I don't know if I could join AA, because I am sex deviate".

There is quite a kerfuffle. "(T)he group conscience began to seethe and boil, and it boiled over. Under no circumstances... could we have such a disgrace among us!"

As Bill put it, "our destiny hung on a razor's edge".

And then:

> (D)ear old Bob looked around, and blandly said, "Isn't it time folks, to ask ourselves, 'What would the Master do in a situation like this?' Would he turn this man away?" And that was the beginning of the AA Tradition that any man who has a drinking problem is a member of AA if

*he says so, not whether we say so. (***The History of Gay People in Alcoholics Anonymous**[5]*)

Next, of course, would come the question of gay special composition groups.

And the earliest record of that comes in 1949 in Boston when Ed S approached Bill and told him that he wanted to start a "specialty" group. Of course, Bill wanted to know what kind of specialty group. And Ed replied, speaking very slowly, "H-o-m-o-s-e-x-u-a-l".

Bill's response was simple, and very much consistent with his non-authoritarian approach to the fellowship and its membership. "Whatever you do to discuss your problems, and to stay sober, if you will go to any lengths to achieve sobriety, please do so."

"So in 1949", Ed concluded, "queer AA came to Boston". (*The History of Gay People*, p. 66)

However, that group did not last and it would take another two decades for official and formal gay groups to be launched. This occurred between 1968 and 1971 in San Francisco, Los Angeles, New York and Washington.

As Audrey Borden tells us:

The first group to fit my modern definition of a gay group… was, in fact, the Friday Night Fell Street Group in San Francisco, established in early 1968. This group was

1. started by gay alcoholics, for gay alcoholics;

2. held in a public venue, rather than a private home; and

3. publicized as a gay meeting, inside and outside of AA.

The Fell Street Group was also one of the first gay groups to appear in the AA World Directory in 1975, and it was eventually listed in the local San Francisco directory as a gay meeting. (The History of Gay People in Alcoholics Anonymous, p. 77)

What must be understood though is that at that time homosexual acts were criminal acts, even between consenting adults in private homes. It took a very progressive Prime Minister in Canada, Pierre Trudeau, to decriminalize homosexual acts in 1967, saying quite simply that "the State has no right in the bedrooms of the nation". And it wouldn't be until 1973 that the American Psychiatric Association removed homosexuality from its *Diagnostic and Statistical Manual of Mental Disorders*.

So there were problems, and not just in AA.

But also in AA, even if we try to pretend otherwise. The pretense that we in AA are perfect, open and accepting could well be called Tradition Thirteen.

Again, going back to Audrey: "In the 1960s, 1970s, and 1980s, gay AA groups and their members were subjected to surveillance, harassment, and other forms of intimidation by some of the more homophobic members of AA… Meetings were invaded in an attempt to shut them down".

Meanwhile efforts were being made to list gay meetings as a separate category in the AA World Directory and in local meeting lists.

The issue of listing gay groups as separate "special purpose" groups in the Directory was first discussed at the General Service Conference in 1973. It turned out to be far too rancorous and the debate was tabled for a year.

It came back in 1974 and turned into a two day debate about listing these special purpose (or special composition) groups. On Wednesday "you could tell that the issue was split right down the middle – pro and con". On the Thursday late in the evening "you could sense that something was happening. Everybody, as it is in AA, had [had] a chance to get it off [his or her] chest". A delegate from Canada then moved to list gay groups in the World Directory. And the motion was passed, virtually unanimously (128 to 2). (The History of Gay People in Alcoholics Anonymous, pp. 93-94).

The battle was over. The issue was first raised with Bill in Boston in 1949 and it was finally resolved in 1974, twenty-five years later.

The first conference or "round-up", organized by an ad hoc group of gay AA members in Northern California, was held in San Francisco in 1976. Notice of the conference was published in the AA Grapevine Calendar and over 200 people attended, some from as far away as Vancouver. Subsequent conferences have drawn up to two thousand people and have been held in places like New York and San Francisco.

Various efforts over the years were made to have a "Conference-approved" pamphlet for LGBTQ members of AA. In 1984 the General Service Conference actually voted **not** to publish a pamphlet for gay and lesbian alcoholics. That decision was eventually overturned and in 1989 AAWS published the pamphlet *"AA and the Gay/Lesbian Alcoholic"*.

By that time there were over three hundred cities in the United States which specifically listed gay and lesbian special composition groups.

We Agnostics as Special Groups

Do we agnostics in AA constitute special composition groups?

The answer is very simple: yes and no.

Let's start with "no".

We AA secularists are not a special group precisely because our primary message in our fellowship is one of inclusivity: that an alcoholic is a member of AA if she so declares regardless of belief or lack of belief. Here is the Agnostic AA Preamble:

> *AA agnostic meetings endeavour to maintain a tradition of free expression, and to conduct a meeting where alcoholics may feel free to express any doubts or disbeliefs they may have, and to share their own personal form of spiritual experience, their search for it, or their rejection of it. In keeping with AA tradition, we do not endorse or oppose any form of religion or atheism. Our only wish is to ensure suffering alcoholics that they can find sobriety in AA without having to accept anyone else's beliefs, or having to deny their own.*

Our primary message in this preamble merely echoes the primary purpose of AA which is "to stay sober and help other alcoholics to achieve sobriety".

Interestingly, the Literature Subcommittee which in 1976 was working on a proposed pamphlet for and by agnostics and atheists in AA felt the same way. "This type of pamphlet does not fall under the category 'special groups of alcoholics' literature but concerns a more fundamental and worldwide problem that has resulted in much misinterpretation of the AA Fellowship."

Indeed. As they explained:

> This pamphlet would affirm in clear and concise fashion that "the only requirement for membership in AA is a desire to stop drinking" and that our founders and the group conscience of the fellowship **does not and has never considered** an alcoholic's spiritual beliefs as **necessarily** relevant to the achievement of healthy and happy sobriety… This pamphlet will probably also help the God believer in AA to understand his/her own spiritual values better, as well as to develop tolerance and understanding of many newcomers to AA. (**History - Proposals to Create a Pamphlet for the Non-Believer / Agnostic / Atheist Alcoholic**[6])

As we shall discuss in Chapter 11, this pamphlet has never been published. And if anything the misinterpretation and misunderstanding of AA within AA has grown rather exponentially in the last four decades.

And now the "yes" answer to we agnostics in AA as a special composition group.

If it is helpful for the secular alcoholic to be distinguished from "the God believer in AA" – which is certainly the case today – then, yes, indeed, her groups and meetings should be listed as "special composition" in the AA World Directory and in Intergroup and Central Office AA meeting lists.

Or vice versa. Just saying.

The times they are a-changing with an ever growing percentage of non-believers in North America. It is hard to predict the "composition" of Alcoholics Anonymous when the time comes for it to celebrate its one hundredth anniversary.

We conclude this chapter with a quote from a talk delivered by Jackie B at the Sedona History Symposium in 2015: "Studying and sharing the history of marginalized people in AA is about looking honestly at our past, not to wring our hands at our failings, but to learn from our mistakes and grow towards greater inclusiveness and effectiveness, like any good AA does in their individual recovery." (**Recovery Plays of Jackie B**[7])

[1] **Special Composition Groups In AA**:
http://www.barefootsworld.net/aaspecialgroups.html

[2] **Key Players in AA History**, Bob K (Toronto, Ontario, AA Agnostica, 2015), p. 209.

[3] **Pass It On** (New York, AAWS, 1984), p. 317.

[4] **A History of Special Interest Groups in AA**:
http://aaagnostica.org/2016/12/15/a-history-of-special-interest-groups-in-aa/

[5] **The History of Gay People in Alcoholics Anonymous**, Audrey Borden (Binghamton, New York, Hawthorn Press, 2007), p. 15.

[6] **History - Proposals to Create a Pamphlet for the Non-Believer / Agnostic / Atheist Alcoholic**: http://aaagnostica.org/wp-content/uploads/2013/06/History-Proposals-to-Create-A-Pamphlet.pdf

[7] **Recovery Plays of Jackie B**:
http://www.recoveryplaysofjackieb.org/about/

Chapter 9:
Back to Basics and Other Religionists

By life-j

Introduction

In a history of secular AA we need to talk about groups and individuals whose purposes are at odds with ours. Some of them are actively fighting inclusion of non-believers as rightful members of AA. Others are simply going about their business promoting their honestly held belief that a god is central to recovery, and that the steps must be worked exactly as Bill Wilson wrote them in 1939.

In his later years, Bill seemed genuinely concerned that the fellowship he had set in motion, and for which he had written the basic text, was becoming increasingly and unduly heavy-handed with the god stuff.

Dr Bob was much more of a Christian than Bill, but they both came from the Oxford Group with its heavy religiosity. And while the non-religious part of AA has finally begun growing and claiming its rightful place within AA it is no wonder that in a heavily religious place like North America there are factions in AA pulling in the opposite direction.

And just like we have our own secular movement, there are religionists who have their own groups, and they have been around for quite some time. Many of these individuals or groups claim to be part of AA, though AA disowns some of them.

Some also choose to distance themselves from AA entirely, and have their own groups, their own meeting schedules, their own literature, and their own Big Book which of course is the first edition. **Alcoholics Victorious**[1], founded in 1948, recognizes Jesus Christ as its "Higher Power" and uses the 12 Steps and the Bible as recovery tools. **Celebrate Recovery**[2] was founded in 1990 and believes that AA is too vague in referring to God as a higher power and promotes a specifically Christ-based 12 Step program ("God" remains in their steps; "as we understood Him" has been removed). Celebrate Recovery claims to have had more than two and half million people complete its program.

These are just two examples.

What all of these "religionist" groups and individuals – both in and out of AA – have in common is the idea that the Big Book is the way to get and stay sober. They treat the Big Book as a Bible and the 12 steps as "sacred" rather than "suggested". Some consider Bill to have written the Big Book with direct inspiration from god, while others simply accept it as an infallible book of instructions. But they're all really based on connection with God. And since there is only one way to get and stay sober, and that involves God, they have little patience for agnostics and atheists. We're simply doing it wrong, and we're destroying AA with our un-godly ways.

Under the circumstances it is hard to not have the same intolerant attitude toward them in turn. It would be nice if we could just have the fundamentalists, the middle-of-the-roaders, and the unbelievers each work the program however they see fit and work together for our common purpose – to help the next suffering alcoholic – but it's just not happening.

We non-believers have never claimed that our way is the only way.

Primary Purpose

The most informative article on these groups that I found, "An Enquiry into Primary Purpose and Back to Basics AA Groups", is on a British site called **AA Cultwatch**[3], The article appears to be well researched, and doesn't seem to suffer much from any bias.

One of these groups, "Primary Purpose", was inspired by Joe & Charlie's Traveling Step Work Circus. Joe McQuany got sober in an insane asylum in 1962, and in 1973 met up with Charlie Parmley who had come to Little Rock, Arkansas to speak at an Al-Anon convention. They found that they both liked to study the Big Book, and around 1977 they began taking a Big Book study program on the road. They also made tapes of their seminars which were widely distributed.

Their study program took off. It was based on the principle that everything an alcoholic needs to know to get and stay sober is in the Big Book.

A special lunch with Joe and Charlie as speakers was organized at the 1980 International AA Convention. A hundred Joe and Charlie tape sets were given away as door prizes for the 1500 people who attended the lunch. "Invitations exploded and within a couple of years, Joe & Charlie were presenting about 36 studies a year worldwide." They were a "reaffirmation" of the belief that the Big Book said everything that needed to be said to the alcoholic with a desire to stop drinking. "Studies have been given in 48 states and most Canadian provinces. Additionally, Australia, New Zealand, England, Scotland, Ireland, Germany, Switzerland, Sweden and the Netherlands have all hosted the Big Book Study seminars with Joe & Charlie… Since 1977, an estimated 200,000 AA Members have experienced the spiritual benefits of these collective studies." (**Big Book Seminar**[4])

A "Primary Purpose" founders' meeting was held on January 26, 1988, in Dallas, organized by Cliff Bishop, one of Charlie's early sponsees. Cliff died in 2016.

> *Our Big Book Study Meetings went pretty well. On occasion, we would have folks from other groups, which were heavy in Discussion Meetings, who would want to share their ES&H with our Group. I'd write a little note to let them know our meetings were to learn what the First One Hundred did that worked so well for them. We were not interested in using meeting time for individuals to share their thoughts or experiences. I would hand them the note and most of the time, they would then join us in our study.*

They were quite into proselytizing too:

> *Those who make up our Group are very active in taking the message of the Big Book into those places where suffering alcoholics wind up seeking shelter and help. We try to get to them before they become "discussionized." (**The Primary Purpose Group of Alcoholics Anonymous**[5])*

For these people it is not about sharing experience, strength and hope, but instead about passing on the exact message of the Big Book. What Bill Wilson wrote with three years of sobriety is, for them, simply the first and the last word.

Joe died on October 25, 2007 and Charlie on April 21, 2011.

Back to Basics

The other main fundamentalist group is Back to Basics. It works much in the same way, but has different origins.

Another determined person, Wally P, launched Back to Basics, with some tapes, in December 1995. He later also published a variety of books, first among them *Back to Basics* in 1998, and that year the first real seminars were held.

B2B groups similar to Primary purpose have sprung up in many places. The two have references to each other, even though they aren't directly associated. Wally P is still going strong, as you can see from his speaking engagement and workshop schedule for 2017 at the website **AA Back to Basics**[6] but he will not be doing any workshops in 2018 in order to focus on writing more books.

The only statistic we have on the number of B2B meetings is from 2009 from AA Cultwatch. At that time there were 130 groups listed in the US. Some of these meetings were also on the pertinent Intergroup schedules while others weren't, either because Intergroup didn't want them, or because the meetings themselves preferred not to be associated directly with AA.

For Primary purpose they showed the following statistics on their growth:

- 2006: Fifty nine groups in six countries;
- 2007: Sixty eight groups in nine countries;
- 2009: One hundred and six groups in eleven countries.

The biggest cause for concern is not the number of groups but rather the individual members of Back to Basics who remain involved in regular AA and push their agenda wherever possible.

It seems to be a common characteristic of these groups that they are heavily invested in the use of study guides with which they teach a specific, firmly in place, fundamentalist version of AA's program. It is about recovering in one way only, by the book exactly, one size fits all, no ESH, no discussion about it, except perhaps discussion here and there about what exactly Bill Wilson meant by one particular passage or another.

It is like bible study all over again.

Dick B

There are other prolific Christian AA spinoff writers. Dick B deserves mention.

There is no doubt where Dick B is coming from. On his web page, **Dick B's Web Site**[7], up front is a plaque with the Big Book on one side, and the Bible on the other. His recovery program is strictly Christian. About the man who introduced him to a new life he tells:

> *When Peter believed, said this man, he walked. When he became afraid, he sank. And it took Jesus to pull him out of the water. I quickly saw that I had a choice – to learn and believe what God had to offer, or to yield my thinking to the seeming disasters the world was offering... So I resolved to go to the Seattle International Convention of Alcoholics Anonymous in 1990 in order to try to find out what role, if any, the Bible had really played in the founding, development, program, and successes of Alcoholics Anonymous.*

And he's a loose cannon for god from there on.

He doesn't mention either Back to Basics or Primary Purpose, so he's not directly affiliated with those groups, and it doesn't appear that he has started a "program" with groups all over the place like the others. But he does refer to the International Christian Recovery Coalition, "An informal, worldwide fellowship of Christians who care about carrying an accurate, effective, message about the role that God, His Son Jesus Christ, and the Bible played in the origins, history, founding, original program, and astonishing successes of the early Alcoholics Anonymous 'Christian fellowship' founded in Akron in 1935."

Dick B mostly has written a lot of books, about 45.

There are titles such as:

• *The Good Book and The Big Book: AA's Roots in the Bible*

• *The Oxford Group & Alcoholics Anonymous: A Design for Living That Works!*

• *Twelve Steps for YOU: Let Our Creator, AA History, and the Big Book be Your Guide*

Oh right, there once was Clarence S – one of the first members of AA, from Cleveland, and though he and Dr. Bob had some early conflicts, basically Clarence taught "Akron style" AA – get down on your knees and pray to your creator for deliverance from alcoholism.

Clarence was a busy circuit speaker, and also wrote books.

It may be that all these fundamentalist circuit speaking, book writing travelling circuses learned their ways from Clarence S.

Circuit speakers are a phenomenon in AA which have an aspect to them which perhaps ought to be described as "personalities before principles". Many carry a relatively down to earth, middle of the road message, while a few do pull AA in a fundamentalist direction.

The Mt Rainier Minority Opinion and the White Paper

While we non-believers are trying to widen the gateway and make AA a bigger tent with room for all, the fundamentalists are doing exactly the opposite. They are trying to narrow down AA as much as they can. They are trying to keep agnostics and atheists out and to deny that we have a right to even be a part of the fellowship. They have in partic-ular been fighting the initiatives within AA to make literature by and for unbelievers and secular AA available.

There are a couple of relatively recent articles of a fundamentalist persuasion, but before we address them let us mention **Gresham's Law and Alcoholics Anonymous**[8], written in 1976 by Tom Powers Sr. and subsequently updated by his son in 1993. It is all about the dire consequences of "watering down AA", as in "strong tea" and "weak tea". "Strong tea good, weak tea bad", as in strong, fundament-alist, original Akron style, Oxford based program, as understood by the author. While originally written a long time ago it appears to have had considerable influence on the fundamentalist movements, and to this day is still widely quoted.

Let's now focus on two other documents.

The **Minority Opinion Appeal to AA Fellowship**[9] (56 pages) from the Mt Rainier Group in Maryland was submitted to the General Service Conference in 2011. Its sole purpose was to block the public-ation of "Conference-approved" literature for, by and about atheists and agnostics in AA. What follows is a slightly abbreviated version of the position of the group, from the first page of the document:

> • *The program of Alcoholics Anonymous is outlined in the Big Book which is our society's basic text. The book gives clear cut directions on how to practice AA's Twelve Steps which are described, in the Foreword to the Twelve Steps and Twelve Traditions, as "a group of principles, spiritual in their nature, which, if practiced as a way of life, can expel the obsession to drink and enable the sufferer to become happily and usefully whole."*

> • *Practicing the Twelve Steps enables alcoholics to develop faith in a Higher Power (or God of one's understanding) that is sufficient to bring about recovery from alcoholism.*

> • *Consequently, any literature which attempts to describe current atheists or agnostics as being "successfully sober" in AA would be deceptive, misleading, and harmful to* **real alcoholics** *attempting to find the power necessary to solve their problem. Such a position is fundamentally opposed to the authentic program of recovery detailed in the Big Book of Alcoholics Anonymous…*

> • *Much of our existing Conference-approved literature is geared toward helping non-believers develop enough faith, in something greater than themselves, to succeed with the program of recovery as it is outlined in the Big Book. Consequently, as the Trustees Literature Committee has concluded in each of the previous six attempts from 1976 to 2006, there is no "need" for additional literature on this subject.*

Does any of this sound familiar?

Has it had an influence on "conventional" AA as a whole?

Well, it was presented at the General Service Conference which meets for a week once a year every spring. The conference consists of roughly 130 members: delegates from 93 AA Areas in North America, 21 trustees of the General Service Board (these trustees –

14 alcoholics and 7 non-alcoholics – are the principal planners and administrators of AA's overall policy and finances, which is about as high-level as it gets in Alcoholics Anonymous) as well as various directors and AA staff. It functions as the active voice and group conscience of the fellowship.

How could it not influence conventional AA?

While the GSC of 2011 did not adopt this minority opinion, it certainly had an influence on conference delegates. A proposed pamphlet for, by and about atheists and agnostics in AA was abandoned yet again and instead the shameful "Many Paths to Spirituality" pamphlet was published in 2014.

Moving on…

The **White Paper**[10] originated in Florida. It is 28 pages long and was written by an old-timer there in 2010.

It is very much consistent with what we have shared earlier in this chapter. First, it places the emphasis on a need for a God, at one point even suggesting that, "Sobriety is not the name of the game, God is". The principle here being that "God could and would if he were sought." If you find god, well you don't need alcohol. Second, it denigrates atheists and agnostics and suggests that we really don't belong in the Fellowship.

Here are two quotes:

> It is time for the pamphlets, the videos, the Grapevine articles, the speeches of Trustees, and overall attitude of our Central Office to acknowledge the authority of the One who responded to the cries of our co-founder, Bill W, and guided us to the most precious spiritual society on this planet. The role of this "Authority" should continuously be referred to instead of slowly eliminating any mention of Him in our publications and speeches. Without this incredible "Power", none of us would have experienced a spiritual awakening and sensed the presence of our Creator…

> One of the policies being advanced by the General Service Office and some of our Trustees regarding expanding our membership is extremely disconcerting. In a not too subtle way, the idea is being advanced that we could make our Fellowship more "inclusive" if we

put "God" in the background and let outsiders think that spirituality in AA was "optional". This would enable so-called "non-believers" to enter AA with the assurance that they could easily keep their current beliefs. I would rather hear about serving beer at meetings than diminishing God's central role.

The author of The White Paper was said to have been Sandy Beach, who died on September 28, 2014 at the age of 83. He was ten weeks away from fifty years of sobriety.

Sandy – his real first name was Richard – was, again, a circuit speaker. A very popular circuit speaker. He "shared to great effect with tens of thousands of fellow alcoholics as one of the nation's most sought-after speakers at conferences, retreats and other gatherings of Alcoholics Anonymous" (**Washington Post**[11]). His talks are also available online at **Stories of Recovery**[12].

What is clear is that both Sandy as a speaker and The White Paper had an influence on AA overall. Remember it was written in 2010. And The White Paper was widely circulated in Toronto in 2011 among the members of the Greater Toronto Area Intergroup. It is fair to say that this paper played a role in the expulsion by the GTAI of the two agnostic groups at the end of May, 2011.

Conclusion

There are many different groups and individuals operating in the fundamentalist field of AA.

Their ascendancy happened around the same time as the publishing of the *Daily Reflections*, most of it a completely shameless piece of god promotion, and around the same time AA began to stagnate. It seems that these people feel certain that the only way forward is more going backwards.

I have no good explanation for why it all came to a head at around the 50 year mark, but Bill Wilson already seemed to think it was inevitable in 1961: "As time passes our book literature has a tendency to get more and more frozen – a tendency for conversion into something like dogma. This is a trait of human nature I am afraid we can do little about. We may as well face the fact that AA will always have its fundamentalists, its absolutists and its relativists."

Well, we certainly do have our fundamentalists, our "religionists" in AA. But shall they rule the Fellowship?

[1] **Alcoholics Victorious**: https://alcoholicsvictorious.org/

[2] **Celebrate Recovery**: http://www.celebraterecovery.com/

[3] **AA Cultwatch**: http://aacultwatch.blogspot.ca/

[4] **Big Book Seminar:** http://bigbookseminar.org/

[5] **The Primary Purpose Group of Alcoholics Anonymous**: http://ppgaadallas.org/

[6] **AA Back to Basics**: http://www.aabacktobasics.org/

[7] **Dick B's Web Site**: http://www.dickb.com/index.html

[8] **Gresham's Law and Alcoholics Anonymous**: http://www.barefootsworld.net/aagreshamslaw.html

[9] **Minority Opinion Appeal To AA Fellowship**: http://aaagnostica.org/wp-content/uploads/2014/09/Minority-Opinion-Appeal-to-AA-Fellowship.pdf

[10] **White Paper**: http://aaagnostica.org/wp-content/uploads/2013/11/White-Paper.pdf

[11] **Washington Post**: https://www.washingtonpost.com/local/with-humor-popular-alcoholics-anonymous-speaker-sandy-beach-saved-lives/2014/12/06/6574f254-7cdb-11e4-9a27-6fdbc612bff8_story.html

[12] **Stories of Recovery**: http://storiesofrecovery.org/SandyB.htm

Chapter 10:
Conformity and Conventional AA

Conventional AA meetings can be both religious and conformist.

Religiosity: There can be a lot of God on placards and in readings and in Conference-approved pamphlets and books on literature tables. And meetings can end with the Lord's Prayer (even though AA claims to be "spiritual not religious"). And this is unfortunately true in most AA meetings in North America.

Conformism: "The adoption of the ideas, attitudes, behavior, etc, of the group to which one belongs".

In too many cases (in meetings or Intergroup) these ideas and attitudes can be pushed on others as the one way. The only way. That can be called authoritarianism: demanding that people agree and denying them the possibility to believe or act as they wish.

Where does all that come from? Is it from the fundamentalist groups and individuals described in an earlier chapter? Is it from the origins of AA in the 1930s in the Christian evangelical pietism of the Oxford Group? Is it merely a feature of tribalism ("loyalty to a political or social group, so that the group is supported unconditionally") which in turn is a part of being human, and in this specific case a part of being a vulnerable and recovering alcoholic in AA?

Or is it all of the above?

In a talk given by Bill Wilson at a General Service Conference in 1965 in New York he declared, "Our very first concern should be with those sufferers that we are still unable to reach". And then he asked, "How much and how often did we fail them?"

Surely some of that failure is a result of the religiosity of, and conformity within, AA.

So let's talk about that.

Religiosity

Let's begin at the beginning. In 1939. A long, long time ago. Bill Wilson and a handful of people he met with regularly had a few years of sobriety and relied upon half a dozen word-of-mouth principles to maintain their sobriety.

Bill remembers: "I split the word-of-mouth program up into smaller pieces... I was surprised that in a short time, perhaps half an hour, I had set down certain principles which, on being, counted, turned out to be twelve in number."

That's where the 12 Steps come from. Bill continues, "For some unaccountable reason, I had moved the idea of God into the Second Step, right up front. Besides I had named God very liberally throughout the other steps. In one of the steps I had even suggested that the newcomer get down on his knees." ("Where Did The Twelve Steps Come From", AA Grapevine, 1953)

And yes, God is mentioned very often in the Steps, even in the edited version published in April, 1939 in *Alcoholics Anonymous: The Story of How More Than One Hundred Men Have Recovered From Alcoholism* (the original title of the book).

Exactly half of the 12 Steps contain a reference to God. The first is a reference to "a Power greater than ourselves" (Step 2), two refer to "God, as we understood Him" (Steps 3 and 11), another two simply say "God" (Steps 5 and 6) and one refers to God as "Him" (Step 7).

That's a lot of God for a few short sentences. But at least the newcomer is no longer told to get down on his knees.

This is a Christian God. An anthropomorphic God ("Him").

An interventionist God. In "How It Works", Chapter 5 of *Alcoholics Anonymous*, the reader is told:

> *(b) That probably no human power could have relieved our alcoholism.*

> *(c) That God could and would if He were sought.*

This is a quite specifically a Christian – and thus a religious – conception of God. Christianity conceives of God as personal and active in the governance of the world. In the Steps, one can have "conscious contact with God" (Step 11) and God can do things such as remove our defects of character and our shortcomings (Steps 6 and 7). This interventionist God ("God could and would if He were sought"), derived from the Oxford Group, is a Christian conception of God.

Thus the "religiosity" of conventional AA.

Never mind the "as you understand Him" part. No matter how hard you try to break away, to escape from the religiosity of AA, you are inevitably driven back to the anthropomorphic and interventionist – Christian and religious – deity of the Big Book and the 12 Steps.

It would be a relief to say that the religiosity of conventional AA ended there, with the Steps and the Big Book some eighty years ago, but it didn't.

In 1990, some fifty years after the Big Book was published, AA published another "Conference-approved" book. This one was called *Daily Reflections*. An excellent review of the book by life-j was published on AA Agnostica on January 17, 2017: **The Daily Reflections**[1].

It is meant for the alcoholic who wishes to begin his or her day with an inspiring reading, something that will be supportive and help him or her to maintain another day of abstinence from alcohol. As life-j reports, the vast majority of the daily reflections have the following script:

> *No matter what the beginning quote, and no matter what the following "reflection" says about that quote, and even no matter whether or not it even says something intelligent, or coherent about that reflection, which is far from always the case – somehow, even if there has been nothing up to that point to warrant it – they invoke god in (usually) the last three lines. Gratitude toward god, or just plain talking about the things god does in the ordinary course of existence.*

In the end, 242 of the 365 daily reflections talk about God. That's two out of three days.

A good number of AA meetings begin with the *Daily Reflections*.

It's just another example of the religiosity of conventional AA. It isn't just what was written in 1939. It's what official AA approved and promoted a half a century after the beginning of Alcoholics Anonymous, and continues to promote today.

The religiosity of AA.

This is certainly something that has been recognized and acknowledged by the high Courts in the United States. They have repeatedly reviewed the evidence at hand and concluded that "a fair reading of the fundamental AA doctrinal writings discloses that their dominant theme is unequivocally religious." (New York Court of Appeals, 1996) You can read more about these court rulings, and their implications, at AA Agnostica: **The Courts, AA and Religion**[2].

When asked about this view of the Courts, the General Service Office will typically say that it can't comment because a Court's opinion is an "outside issue". No it's not.

It's an inside issue.

Conformity

So, the newcomer has finally reached – or is getting close to reaching – the end of her drinking and she decides to go to an AA meeting.

What she will probably see first, because this is the case in the vast majority of AA meetings, is a very large placard at the front of the room with the 12 Steps. "Power… God… God… God… Him… God… Him…"

A large number of AA meetings begin with a reading of "How It Works". So the 12 Steps will be read for everybody present, in case they have never yet heard them, as they were written three quarters of a century ago. Again: "Power… God… God… God… Him… God… Him…"

And here are a few other quotes from that reading:

> *Rarely have we seen a person fail who has thoroughly followed our path. Those who do not recover are people who cannot or will not completely give themselves to this simple program, usually men and women who are constitutionally incapable of being honest with themselves…*

> *Remember that we deal with alcohol – cunning, baffling, powerful! Without help it is too much for us. But there is One who has all power – that One is God. May you find Him now!*

But there is a surprise coming. "How It Works" always ends with the two points mentioned in the previous section:

> *(b) That probably no human power could have relieved our alcoholism.*

(c) That God could and would if He were sought.

And the surprise? Everyone in the room joins in and chants the last point: "That God could and would if He were sought!"

The meeting goes on. Often it will be a speaker who will share "what it was like, what happened and what it is like now". Or the celebration of a sobriety anniversary. Or a discussion of various topics. Sometimes if the audience is large enough it will break into groups for discussions. There is a variety of fellowship meeting formats.

But it's how it ends…

Today, across North America, many meetings end with the Lord's Prayer.

All those present will stand up and reach out to one another, and hold hands. Presumably that includes the newcomer. And then the Chair of the meeting will say something like, "Who's in charge?" And then everyone recites the Lord's Prayer:

> *Our Father who art in heaven, hallowed be thy name. Thy kingdom come. Thy will be done on earth, as it is in heaven. Give us this day our daily bread, and forgive us our trespasses, as we forgive those who trespass against us, and lead us not into temptation, but deliver us from evil. For thine is the kingdom, the power, and the glory, For ever and ever. Amen.*

That is pretty much, give or take a point here or there, a conventional AA meeting.

The newcomer in AA is a very vulnerable human being.

And "those who do not recover are people who cannot or will not completely give themselves to this simple program…"

And this "simple program" will be coming at her from all different directions within conventional AA. The Big Book, on the Literature table. The 12 Steps as published in 1939 and included in every single pamphlet on the Literature table. And God, who "could and would if He were sought".

Conventional AA can be groupings of rather dogmatic women and men. These ideas and attitudes can be pushed on the newcomer as the one way. The only way.

Bill Wilson saw it coming.

"It is a historical fact," he said, "that practically all groupings of men and women tend to become dogmatic. Their beliefs and practices harden and sometimes freeze. This is a natural and almost inevitable process." (**Responsibility is Our Theme**[3])

It is actually quite astonishing and dreadful how many people believe that everything you need to know about alcoholism, and recovery from alcoholism, is in the first 164 pages of *Alcoholics Anonymous*. These people, more than anything or anyone else, can make going to conventional AA meetings very difficult.

It is not our goal to rewrite the Big Book.

It is an historical document. It was published in 1939. It was the wisdom of a handful of white, middle-class, and mostly Christian, men. It was profoundly influenced by the Oxford Group, which was a Christian "evangelical pietist" movement. What does that mean? The "evangelical" part involves fervor for carrying the message of the gift of an omnipotent God. The "pietist" part expresses an aversion to the idea that humans are sufficient unto themselves. These ideas blossomed in the mid-1930s and were present in the Oxford Group and influenced a nascent AA. That's where God and a higher Power emerged in AA. That's what directly fed the idea that "probably no human power" could relieve our alcoholism and that we alcoholics, in particular, are riddled with character defects. Beyond all that *Alcoholics Anonymous* has two horrible chapters: "To Wives", which is incredibly disrespectful of women, and "We Agnostics", which is incredibly disrespectful of those not saddled by a Christian faith or religion.

Still, it is not our goal to rewrite the Big Book.

We can learn in other ways and read other more contemporary (mostly "non-Conference-approved") literature. That is an obvious and rather inevitable way forward.

And the 12 Step program as written in 1939 is neither the best nor the only way to sobriety. The best way is whatever works for the recovering alcoholic. One of the more important moments in my own recovery was the discovery of William White, the author of *Slaying the Dragon: The History of Addiction Treatment and Recovery in America*, and his commitment to the celebration of all paths to recovery.

It opened the door. It allowed me to move forward in different ways, at the same time, without hesitation. It provided me with the understanding that we all have our own unique recoveries, even if we use a similar "path" or "road" to recovery. Most alcoholics have problems – psychological, emotional, mental – other than alcoholism. Indeed over sixty percent of AA members receive outside treatment for concurrent disorders.

So, in the end, it makes perfect sense that each path to recovery is unique and ought to be celebrated.

It also makes perfect sense that the 12 Steps as written in 1939 are neither the best nor the only path to recovery. In fact, with "God", "Him" or "Power" in six of the 12 Steps, and with the way in which they reflect an odd and antiquated "evangelical pietism" of the Oxford group in 1930s, the Steps can indeed seem a tad outdated.

Which is not to say that the Steps can't be used and/or adapted to be a relevant, crucial and often life-changing path to sobriety, which they are for many people.

That's not the problem. The problem is an authoritarian approach in conventional AA that pushes the 12 Steps as written, and the Big Book, and the need for a God "who could and would if He were sought", as the sole legitimate path to recovery from alcoholism.

That is not rare in AA. That is quite common in conventional AA.

Just get used to it? No thank you.

As Bill Wilson put it, "Simply because we have convictions that work very well for us, it becomes quite easy to assume that we have all of the truth. Whenever this brand of arrogance develops we are sure to become aggressive. We demand agreement with us. We play God."

We have seen the aggression. We have seen the dogmatism. We have seen those who "play God" in Alcoholics Anonymous.

And as Bill concludes, "This isn't good dogma. This is very bad dogma. It could be especially destructive for us of AA to indulge in this sort of thing." (Responsibility is Our Theme)

Indeed. It may well be the most prevalent and harmful element in AA today.

[1] **The Daily Reflections**: http://aaagnostica.org/2017/01/19/the-daily-reflections/

[2] **The Courts, AA and Religion**: http://aaagnostica.org/2012/05/27/the-courts-aa-and-religion/

[3] **Responsibility is Our Theme**: http://aaagnostica.org/2012/10/07/responsibility-is-our-theme/

Chapter 11:
Conference-approved Literature

More than forty years ago, Ed and Paula, two members of an AA trustees Literature Sub-Committee, wrote that a pamphlet written by and for agnostics and atheists in AA was "needed to assure non-believers that they are not merely deviants, but full, participating members in the AA Fellowship without qualification."

To date, that Conference-approved pamphlet has never been published.

Never. Been. Published.

And this is in spite of at least half a dozen major efforts over the last four decades.

If anything, we agnostics in AA feel like deviants and outcasts in AA more now than ever before, even dating back eighty years when AA was founded in 1935.

But let's start at the beginning with the origins of these requests for AA literature for non-believers. Much of what follows comes from the following document: **History - Proposals to Create a Pamphlet for the Non-Believer / Agnostic / Atheist Alcoholic**[1].

A "Conference-approved" pamphlet for agnostics and atheists in AA was first proposed in 1975.

The proposal was the result of a letter from Al L, an AA member in Florida, who asked the Trustees' Literature Committee to consider publishing such a pamphlet.

(The trustees of AA consist of 14 alcoholics and 7 non-alcoholics. These trustees are the principal planners and administrators of AA's overall policy and finances, which is about as high-level as it gets in Alcoholics Anonymous.)

This is what Al wrote:

> I'm a happy non-belligerent agnostic. I feel that many non-believers miss the AA boat before they find out that they are also welcome. The "God bit" frightens then off before they learn that their spiritual beliefs or non-beliefs need not deprive them of the blessings of AA.

Is it possible for the "powers that be" in AA to publish a pamphlet designed specifically for agnostics? I don't mean the Big Book's version – Chapter IV We Agnostics – that doesn't make sense to me. Never did...

Many agnostics believe at first that AA, with all of its "Let God Do It" and "That one is God, may you find him now" is really a thinly veiled attempt to shove "religion" down their throats. You and I of course know that isn't the case...

I would not advise that such a pamphlet for agnostics imply or infer that "God" will get you sooner or later or that you will necessarily come to believe in the power of prayer or that you must "turn it over."

My logic, common sense and dedication to AA keeps me sober – and I don't think the non-spiritual have been given a fair shake.

There's much of course in Al's letter that makes a great deal of sense. Nonbelievers in AA have definitely not been given a "fair shake" over the years.

After all, what does an agnostic do when an interventionist God appears a total of six times in the 12 Steps? What does he or she do when the AA meeting – in a church basement, no less – ends with the Lord's Prayer?

It is important to note that Al is asking for a pamphlet that lets go of the idea that God is necessary for recovery. The pamphlet would acknowledge straight out that agnostics and atheists can and, quite commonly, do get sober and maintain their sobriety within AA – and do that without God.

To its credit, the Literature Committee was open to the idea, at least initially. The trustees thought Al's proposal was important and in February 1976 they appointed a two-member subcommittee to study the issue and report back. Specifically, "The Committee recommended that the preparation of a pamphlet for Agnostics be studied by a sub-committee consisting of Ed S and Paula C."

After four months, in July 1976, these two submitted a preliminary report strongly recommending the publication of this pamphlet. Here is what the report recommended, divided into three parts:

A. Reasons for the pamphlet

This pamphlet is vitally needed to carry the message to both newcomers and old timers.

Alcoholics Anonymous, despite first appearances, is neither sectarian nor religious, and is open to all alcoholics of every persuasion or non-persuasion. The number of nonbelievers in the program, or who need the AA program but are discouraged by its theism, may be more substantial than is probably realized.

The chapter "To the Agnostic" in the Big Book is fine as a start but more material is needed to assure nonbelievers that they are not merely deviants, but full, participating members in the AA Fellowship without qualification.

This pamphlet will probably also help the God believer in AA to understand his/her own spiritual values better, as well as to develop tolerance and understanding of many newcomers to AA.

The pamphlet would affirm in clear and concise fashion that "the only requirement for membership in AA is a desire to stop drinking" and that our founders and the group conscience of the fellowship does not and has never considered an alcoholic's spiritual beliefs as necessarily relevant to the achievement of healthy and happy sobriety.

B. A draft should begin as soon as possible

The sub-committee will collect material from extant literature including the Grapevine.

If it appears that this pamphlet geared to the agnostic and/or atheist will not achieve the aims listed above, then it will be discontinued by the Committee at this time.

C. This type of pamphlet does not fall under the category "special groups of alcoholics" literature

It concerns a more fundamental and worldwide problem that has resulted in much misinterpretation of the AA Fellowship.

This last point is very important.

What the subcommittee is saying with this last point is that what AA needs to do with this pamphlet is affirm that sobriety is indeed possible in AA without an interventionist God. Ultimately, that is the only way that it is possible for agnostics and atheists to participate in AA as "full, participating members in the AA Fellowship without qualification". It is the recognition of the fact that "our founders and the group conscience of the fellowship does not and has never considered an alcoholic's spiritual beliefs as necessarily relevant to the achievement of healthy and happy sobriety".

Of course, try telling that to some of "our more religious members".

In August 1976, the trustees' Literature Committee reviewed the two-page report. It suggested that the subcommittee now write a new version of their recommendations in greater detail and present it to the 1977 Conference Committee on Literature before further action is taken on its preparation.

And here, unfortunately, is where light turns to darkness.

The Committee reviewed the revised report in October of 1976.

And turfed it.

Moreover, the trustees Literature Committee did a complete reversal and "decided not to ask the 1977 Conference Literature Committee to consider a pamphlet for agnostics/atheists".

(The Conference meets for a week once a year every spring. It consists of roughly 130 members: delegates from 93 Conference areas in North America, trustees of the General Service Board, and various directors and AA staff. It functions as the active voice and group conscience of the fellowship. All official AA literature must be "Conference-approved".)

To this day, even after "an exhaustive search," a copy of the subcommittee's final report has never been found.

What we do know, however, is that the effort to get a pamphlet for, about and by agnostics in AA continued on and on and on, into the 80s, 90s and, indeed, into the new millennium.

Let's look at what happened in the eighties.

Apparently Ed – the Ed mentioned above, now a former AA trustee – was not the kind of person who gives up simply because of adversity. He wrote a letter in October of 1981 which read, in part:

> *Even though it would not be a best seller, could we have a pamphlet written by an agnostic or atheist for those who have trouble believing? Possible title: "Came Not to Believe".*

In January 1982 "the committee declined to recommend the publication of a pamphlet intended for agnostics or atheists who have trouble believing".

No reason was offered.

Later that decade, in the spring of 1989, the idea of a pamphlet for those "who have trouble believing" finally made it to the General Service Conference.

At least some of the interest in such a pamphlet was generated by an article in the AA Grapevine in October of 1987 called: "Is There Room Enough in AA?" In the article, J L from Oakland, California writes about how, as an atheist with many years of sobriety, he feels muzzled in the rooms of AA:

> *I hear so little from atheists in AA because those of us who do not believe in God keep quiet about it. I have done so partly out of timidity and partly to avoid the comment that the admission of atheism frequently brings: that I will someday believe or I will get drunk.*

Does that sound familiar to anyone?

At any rate, the article prompted a letter from Jack M. to the General Service Office dated February 1, 1989.

At the time Jack had some thirteen years of sobriety in AA, and one of his comments picks up on the theme of the Grapevine article:

> *I can't understand why (believers) hardly ever tire of trying to convince or persuade nonbelievers to change, particularly in AA which is a program of attraction,*

because the thought of trying to persuade a believer to change never even enters my mind.

He goes on to say:

> *There just doesn't seem to be any AA General Service Conference-approved literature written specifically for the non-believer. Is such a project under way? ...A collection of encouraging words would not have to be adversarial, antagonistic, cogent, defensive, patronizing or persuasive. A foreword could even be included which would explain the apparent conflict, at least to some newcomers, between the statement in our preamble regarding AA not being allied with any sect, denomination, organization or institution and the fact that we all rise... and recite the prayer beginning Our Father at the close of each meeting. The foreword could also contain a clear statement that belief in a higher power is not at any time a requirement for membership or for getting and staying sober.*

Another letter had also been written to the General Service Office in 1989 and that one was by Tom M of Florida.

He writes of the many atheists who have gotten and stayed sober within the rooms of AA. "We believe," he says, "that we have accumulated experiences that can give hope, strength, and comfort to newly sober people in AA who are of the agnostic or atheistic persuasion".

He goes on to say:

> *To declare your agnosticism or atheism at many meetings (at least in this part of the country) brings upon oneself knowing stares and sometimes repudiation from someone in the group. Now, I personally don't have this problem anymore. My longevity in sobriety is given respect, but I am still thought of as a paradox or oddball. I can handle that just fine, now. The question that bothers me, is that "Can a newly sober agnostic or atheist handle being treated as an oddball?" Many cannot.*

These letters, and others, were duly considered by the trustees' Literature Committee which made a recommendation "for some sort of spiritual literature in response to requests from atheists and agnostics".

Not a chance.

As noted above, the spring 1989 General Service Conference considered the request. And it blew the idea right out of the water.

It "did not see a sufficient need to take action".

And so it goes. To put it mildly, the request for what is sometimes described as life-saving literature for the non-believing alcoholic was treated cavalierly.

And there were further requests. A least half a dozen requests were made between 1976 and 2006 and each and every one was rejected.

———

Still there was some hope. And more requests would come after 2006. But perhaps the hope for a pamphlet for and by agnostics and atheists ended in 2011 when the Mount Rainier Group, from Maryland, presented its **Minority Opinion Appeal to AA Fellowship**[2] to that year's General Service Conference.

It was a 57 page appeal devoted to trashing the idea of literature for non-believers. Here is a typical quote from the Opinion Appeal:

> *Any literature which attempts to describe current atheists or agnostics as being "successfully sober" in AA would be deceptive, misleading, and harmful to **real alcoholics** attempting to find the power necessary to solve their problem… (A)ttempts to provide information approved by AAWS about how individuals or groups of people have stayed "successfully sober in Alcoholics Anonymous" without relying upon a Power greater than themselves, or God as we understood him, is in direct opposition to the AA message as it is laid out in the first 164 pages of the big book, and, therefore, threatens the integrity of our "**common solution**" (**Big Book, p. 17**).*

Of course, underlying all of this is Big Book fundamentalism. It treats Alcoholics Anonymous, published in 1939, as the Bible for alcoholics.

And of course (a) everything in the book is one hundred and ten percent accurate and (b) we have learned nothing since its publication.

This appeal by the Mount Rainier group was rejected by the General Service Conference. Nevertheless enough delegates at the Conference supported it that it became obvious that a pamphlet by and for non-believers, as it was described way back in 1976, was not going to happen.

And it didn't.

––––––––

The GSO and the General Service Conference need to take a large degree of responsibility for what is happening in AA today.

And that has a great deal to do with "Conference-approved" literature.

The term "Conference-approved" is a disaster. Whether it is the purpose of the term or not it trashes or at the very least trivializes all other recovery related literature. It narrows the gateway. It results in the imposition of an extraordinarily small collection of literature on those in AA.

Moreover, it is the celebration of one form of recovery – which is all about God and the 12 Step program as written in 1939 – and thus the denial of other paths to recovery from alcoholism. It is one of the elements that have inevitably led to the religiosity, conformity and authoritarianism so common and so prevalent today in conventional AA.

Bob Pearson, a retired Manager of the General Service Office from 1974 to 1984, talked about the "growing rigidity" of AA. In particular he talked about "prohibiting non-Conference-approved literature, i.e., 'banning books;' (and) laying more and more rules on groups and members". (General Service Conference, April 26, 1986)

Prohibiting. Banning. What he is talking about is censorship.

Most AA meetings have literature tables. Invariably the only literature – books and pamphlets – found on these tables is "Conference-approved". Why? Because this literature is acquired from Intergroups and Central Offices which only have "Conference-approved" literature, which they have purchased from AA World Services, which in turn only sells books and pamphlets which it has published and which have been designated "Conference-approved". Indeed, the GSO will tell you that "Conference approval assures us that a piece of literature represents solid AA experience".

Try to put something else on those tables and it will invariably be refused.

Pearson's "prohibition of non-Conference-approved literature". It's very common in AA. It's invoked by the term itself. We even saw it, of all places, in the planning of the Santa Monica convention for we agnostics, atheists and freethinkers in AA.

And it is about religiosity and conformity.

With few exceptions – the book *Living Sober*, published in 1975, is one – those traits will be found in much of the "Conference-approved" literature.

Did you know that every "Conference-approved" pamphlet contains the 12 Steps, as written in 1939?

Let's take a look at a pamphlet published by AA World Services in 2014, "Many Paths to Spirituality", a "Conference-approved" pamphlet that was supposed to at least be cordial towards atheists and agnostics in AA.

In his review of the pamphlet, Chris G writes: "The words 'atheist' and 'agnostic' are used exactly three times each in the pamphlet. 'God' is used nine times. 'Higher power' appears thirteen times. Variations on 'pray' are there nine times. (**The Many Paths to Spirituality Pamphlet**[3]) The pamphlet is in essence a variation of Chapter Four of *Alcoholics Anonymous*.

At one point in the pamphlet, a Jew says: "Today I can even recite the Lord's Prayer without feeling guilty since it was pointed out to me in 'How it Works' that I have to go to any length to get and stay sober." It is shocking that the 130 or so voting men and women at the 2014 General Service Conference thought that this was, in any way, an acceptable thing to share within the fellowship of AA. It is disrespectful towards Jews. It tells the reader that the Lord's Prayer belongs in AA and is an integral part of achieving and maintaining sobriety. It is so wrong and unacceptable.

So how does the pamphlet end? In the second last paragraph an atheist supposedly says: "I have been able to do the Steps just as they are written in the Big Book." This is clearly an admonishment to others not to change the Steps as written in 1939. It is a message that if you want to get sober you have to crawl back into the world of middle class white men in the 1930s and get sober the way they did or at least the way a few of them did, with the Steps "just as they are written in the Big Book".

That's the whole point of the pamphlet. There aren't "Many Paths". No Sir: there is "One Way".

While the "Many Paths to Spirituality" pamphlet mentions atheists and agnostics, it actually demonstrates the religiosity and conformity expected within the fellowship.

It in no way at all legitimizes the presence in AA of those of us who are and remain sober as a result of resources that do not in any way include a "God". Nor has it – in the least – made traditional meetings more accepting of, and open to, non-believers. And nobody has ever yet heard a non-believer newcomer say that because she has read the "Many Paths" pamphlet, she now feels welcomed with open arms in AA.

A Conference-approved pamphlet for and by atheists and agnostics has never been published.

Never. Been. Published.

The reason is rather straightforward: the members of the General Service Conference are simply not prepared to concede that some women and men in AA do get and stay sober without a Higher Power, whom many choose to call God.

––––––

Bill Wilson at the General Service Conference in New York in 1965 said: "Research has already come up with significant and helpful findings. And research will do far more."

So why is there so little interest in AA in what science and research has told us over the years about alcoholism and recovery from alcoholism and addiction?

AA has published one "Conference-approved" pamphlet on medications and it is called "The AA Member – Medications and Other Drugs". It was updated in 2011 and originally published in 1984. But it is not even about alcoholism or addiction but rather about mental illnesses and a few other chronic physiological illnesses.

Why does the fellowship of AA not care about "significant and helpful findings" that science has and will and may yet come up with on the subject of alcoholism and addiction?

94

To its credit, the AA Grapevine, AA's monthly "meeting in print", has a section called "Alcoholism at Large" which offers this information and a caveat:

> *The purpose of these pages is to offer information that may further readers' understanding of the medical, legal and social aspects of alcoholism; the severity and international scope of the illness; and the worldwide efforts being made to combat it. Publication here does not imply endorsement or affiliation. AA does not conduct or participate in research, nor does it hold any opinion on research by others.*

That's all wonderful, even the caveat.

But AA has all kinds of committees.

Why doesn't the GSO launch a Science Committee?

It could simply keep those of us who are interested up to date with contemporary and scientific research into understanding and dealing with alcoholism. No endorsements or opinions necessary. Isn't that something that should rather obviously and automatically be done by an organization, a fellowship, committed and devoted to helping those who reach out for help in dealing with alcoholism?

But no, none of it. Because all you need to know about recovery from alcoholism is in the Big Book and in "Conference-approved" literature. Because the sacred program of recovery is the 12 Steps – with "God", "Him" or "Power" in six of the twelve – as written in 1939.

Bob Pearson called it "rigidity". He continued, "In this trend toward rigidity, we are drifting farther and farther away from our co- founders".

With its increasing rigidity ("very bad dogma" as Bill described it), Alcoholics Anonymous is clearly drifting farther and farther away from the very soul of the fellowship as it was understood by its co-founders, and that is the ability of Alcoholics Anonymous to genuinely and capably realize its primary purpose and its Responsibility Declaration.

Pearson concluded, "Bill, in particular, must be spinning in his grave".

[1] **History - Proposals to Create a Pamphlet for the Non-Believer / Agnostic / Atheist Alcoholic**: http://aaagnostica.org/wp-content/uploads/2013/06/History-Proposals-to-Create-A-Pamphlet.pdf

[2] **Minority Appeal to AA Fellowship**: http://aaagnostica.org/wp-content/uploads/2014/09/Minority-Opinion-Appeal-to-AA-Fellowship.pdf

[3] **The Many Paths to Spirituality Pamphlet**: http://aaagnostica.org/2014/08/13/the-many-paths-to-spirituality-pamphlet/

Part Three:
Moving Forward

Chapter 12:
Literature for We Agnostics

A few years ago, there was almost nothing for secular alcoholics in AA to read. In fact, before 2010 only a few such books had been published, and one of them had been out of print for a number of years.

That book was called *The Alternative 12 Steps: A Secular Guide to Recovery*. It had been written by two women and published in 1991 in the United States.

The book is quite remarkable. At the time there was no "secular movement" within the fellowship of Alcoholics Anonymous. There were perhaps two dozen agnostic AA meetings worldwide. So Martha and Arlys were not inspired by an outside source; it wasn't because they were encouraged by others that they wrote and published the book. They wrote it based on their own personal convictions and it was published simply to support others who might also find a secular version of the 12 Steps to be helpful in their recoveries from alcoholism.

We repeat: Published in 1991. Bravo Arlys and Martha!

Another two early books that were written by and for atheists in AA were also written by women.

In 2010 *My Name is Lillian and I'm an Alcoholic (and an Atheist): How I got and stayed sober in AA without all that God stuff* was published, but only as an eBook. The chapters in the book are taken from her shares in a three year email AA meeting from 2006 to 2008. It is really quite a special book, a special eBook.

In 2011 Marya Hornbacher's *Waiting: A Nonbeliever's Higher Power* was published. Marya played a very special role in the first convention for we agnostics, atheists and freethinkers in AA in Santa Monica by being one of the three keynote speakers. She was an excellent speaker. Marya also wrote the foreword for *Do Tell! Stories by Atheists and Agnostics in AA*, which is one of books previewed below.

A British author, Vince Hawkins, also wrote a book in 2011, a book which was self-published, *An Atheists Guide to Alcoholics Anonymous*.

And then – beginning in 2013 – there would be an absolute explosion of books for non-believers in AA.

AA Agnostica published six books between 2013 and 2015. One of them – the very special *Key Players in AA History* by Bob K – is not included in the list below simply because it is not aimed specifically at dealing with the issue of secularism in AA. And we are now in the process of publishing two more, one of which is this one, the one in your hands, *A History of Agnostics in AA*. The other will be by Thomas B, a veteran with some 44 years of sobriety who has written a number of articles for both AA Agnostica and AA Beyond Belief, and is now working on a memoir which will be called: *Each Breath a Gift, A Story of Continuing Recovery*. Five books published by AA Agnostica are included in this chapter, including the Second Edition of *The Alternative 12 Steps*.

Another publication of historical import took place in 2013 and that was the publication of the first ever book of secular daily reflections for non-believers in recovery: *Beyond Belief: Agnostic Musings for 12 Step Life*.

Some history: the very first book of daily reflections was called *Twenty-Fours a Day* and was written by Richmond Walker, a member in 1942 of the first AA group in Boston, and it was put together as a book in 1948. It became very popular and sales quickly reached 10,000 copies a year. Overwhelmed, Richmond offered the book to the AA New York Office in 1953. They refused. "Hazelden offered to publish and distribute the book in 1954. It is still widely used by AA members and groups today, with over eight million copies sold." (**Barefoot's World**[1])

And the book is all about "practicing the presence of God". Like the co-founders of AA, Bill and Dr. Bob, Richmond had initially gotten sober in the Oxford Group. "For those who would like to bring modern AA back closer to Oxford Group beliefs and practices, *Twenty-Four Hours a Day* is the most strongly Oxford-Group-oriented work written by an early AA author." (Barefoot's World) With 22 years of sobriety, Richmond Walker died on March 25, 1965.

And of course his is not the only Godly book. We have already written about AA's Conference-approved *Daily Reflections*, published in 1990. Both books are all about pedalling AA backward rather than forward, back to a form of evangelical pietism ("God could and would if he were sought") that was part of, but certainly not exclusive to, the

Oxford Group. Remember, God is mentioned in two out of the three of the *Daily Reflections*.

Both of these books, *Twenty-Four Hours a Day* and *Daily Reflections* – which currently has sales of approximately 150,000 copies a year – have no doubt had an impact upon the dogmatization of conventional AA.

So what to do?

Well, start by getting something else. There are many non-Conference-approved books that are quite good, including the books listed below.

And for daily reflections, how about *365 Tao: Daily Meditations*? And by all means consider purchasing a copy of *Beyond Belief*.

So far we've listed earlier secular books for we agnostics in AA. We've touched on books published by AA Agnostic between 2013 and 2015, we've talked about Beyond Belief, and we will mention one more. It is called *A Freethinker in AA* and is by a rather prolific author, John Lauritsen, who has his own website that includes a section called **Alcoholism: Recovery without Religiosity**[2]. But John's secular writings about AA go a long way back. One is a document that was written on an Olympia manual typewriter and circulated by John in New York City in 1976: **A Proposal to Eliminate the Lord's Prayer from AA Meetings**[3].

It was re-posted again on AA Agnostica in 2011. John recently informed us that by the end of the twentieth century, most AA meetings in NYC had substituted the Serenity Prayer for the Lord's Prayer, so perhaps his proposal, and certainly the growth of secular AA meetings in the city, has had an impact.

What follows are brief summaries of ten of the first books published for agnostics and atheists in AA. Every one of these books has either a review or a Chapter (often a Foreword or an Introduction) on AA Agnostica. They can be accessed by using the Search function on the top of the Home Page of the website. In brackets after each is the specific source for each book's summary (either AA Agnostica, a website for AA Agnostica books called **Recovery 101**[4], or Amazon – which is also a place where all of these books may be purchased).

***

The Alternative 12 Steps: A Secular Guide to Recovery – Martha Cleveland and Arlys G. (First Edition in March 1991, Second Edition published by AA Agnostica on July 15, 2014.)

In 1991, two women were successfully working the 12-Step program… and they were atheists. They knew the program worked, and translated the Steps into secular terms. This ground-breaking book – as valuable today as it was when it was first written – is their sharing of this secular interpretation. In *The Alternative 12 Steps: A Secular Guide to Recovery*, Martha Cleveland and Arlys G. show how the 12-Step program can be interpreted and worked by those who do not believe in an interventionist deity. At the same time the authors conscientiously maintain the intention and integrity of the program – its values, scope and depth. A chapter is devoted to each Step. The language is clear, engaging and personal. The Foreword to this Second Edition of the book begins with a striking quote from Chapter Three which captures the essence of both the book and the 12 Steps: "We can learn the universal, generic pattern of life's dance from the 12 Steps. But in our individual dance of life, we choose our own music and dance our own dance." This is a unique, inspiring and helpful book for anyone – regardless of belief or lack of belief – who would like to work AA's suggested 12 Step recovery program. (Recovery 101)

My Name is Lillian and I'm an Alcoholic (and an Atheist): How I got and stayed sober in AA without all that God stuff – Lillian Sober-Atheist. (Self-published as an eBook on October 15, 2010.)

After 20 years of drinking, at 36 years of age, Lillian found her way into AA and got sober. That was late last century. She's an atheist, she's a New Yorker. And this book, a 2010 gift to the Fellowship, is one of the pioneering resources that a nonbeliever in AA can latch onto. *My Name is Lillian* (the author's pen-name) spans three years of what she calls "one side of a conversation about sobriety". As an AA member Lillian participates in an email AA meeting from Monday February 6, 2006 to Monday October 18th, 2008. We get to tag along and you and I are going to learn a thing or two about Lillian, and if we're lucky, ourselves as well. How you consume the book is up to you. You can marathon through the book in a weekend or savor it a few pages a week until completed. Alternatively, you can just open it randomly and read a few pages and reflect on them. *My Name is Lillian* isn't opinion, criticism or analysis of AA; it's 100% personal journey so there's nothing to disagree with, just a few things that any open-minded reader could learn from to enrich her or his own life. You can get it online for less than a latte. (AA Agnostica, review by Joe C)

———

Waiting: A Nonbeliever's Higher Power – Marya Hornbacher. (Published by Hazelden on April 21, 2011.)

Waiting: A Nonbeliever's Higher Power is refreshing and a joy to read. Hornbacher is quite simply a gifted and humble writer whose earlier writing includes books on her own struggles with anorexia and bulimia, bipolar disorder as well as last year's well-received *Sane: Mental Illness, Addiction and the 12 Steps*. She is a freelance journalist, Pulitzer Prize nominee, novelist, and poet. The wisdom and compassion contained in the pages of *Waiting: A Nonbeliever's Higher Power* cannot help but guide the reader toward a renewed and deeper understanding of a spiritual life which she emphasizes exists right here, right now, in this world. As my atheist wife has said with playful irony, "This book is a Godsend!" (AA Agnostica, review by John M)

———

An Atheists Unofficial Guide to AA – Vince Hawkins. (Self-published on October 28, 2011.)

I am an atheist alcoholic who believes that many people who could be saved from drink by AA do not embrace the fellowship because they are put off by a higher power understood as "God." I have written a book which tweaks the Steps and demonstrates that it is not necessary to believe in a god to follow the program. The idea is to widen the AA net to catch people who would otherwise not be saved. (AA Agnostica article by Vince Hawkins)

———

Beyond Belief: Agnostic Musings for 12 Step Life – Joe C (Published by Rebellion Dogs Publishing on January 21, 2013)

Finally! A daily reflection book for nonbelievers, freethinkers and everyone. *Beyond Belief: Agnostic Musings for 12 Step Life* offers 365 quips for every alcoholic/addict. Drawing on quotes from writers, skeptics, entertainers, economists, religious leaders, philosophers, psychologists and varied recovery fellowship literature, *Beyond Belief* neither canonizes nor vilifies any school of recovery thought. Where else would you find Sam Harris followed by Mother Teresa, Bill Wilson followed with Anais Nin, a doctor's opinion by Dr. Seuss or a spiritual perspective from Albert Einstein? *Beyond Belief* takes a secular look at our recovery culture with help from the classic thinkers of the ages and the wisdom in and around the rooms. (AA Agnostica, review by Carol M)

———

The Little Book: A Collection of Alternative 12 Steps – Roger C. (Published by AA Agnostica on February 20, 2013.)

The unstated goal of *The Little Book* is to widen the gateway of AA so that all who suffer might pass through, regardless of belief or lack of belief. The book presents the 12 Step program of recovery in a way that reflects and respects the diversity of culture, gender, religion and lack of religion within today's worldwide recovery community. The first part consists of 20 alternative versions of the 12 Steps which were originally published in 1939 in the "Big Book," *Alcoholics Anonymous.* In the second major part of the book, four secular interpretations of the original 12 Steps are presented, one Step at a time. These inter-pretations are provided by well known authors Gabor Maté (*In the Realm of Hungry Ghosts*), Stephanie Covington (*A Woman's Way Through the Twelve Steps*), Thérèse Jacobs-Stewart (*Mindfulness and the 12 Steps*) and Allen Berger (*12 Smart Things to Do When the Booze and Drugs Are Gone*). The last part of the book contains an insightful essay, "The Origins of the 12 Steps." In its inclusivity and unqualified respect for diversity and difference, The Little Book para-doxically represents both a challenge to AA while anchored in the very best of its history and traditions. (Recovery 101)

———

Don't Tell: Stories and essays by agnostics and atheists in AA – Edited by Roger C. (Published by AA Agnostica on April 20, 2014.)

Don't Tell contains a total of 64 stories and essays mostly by agnostics and atheists in AA originally posted on AA Agnostica, most often on Sunday mornings, over the last almost three years. These were written by over thirty men and women from almost as many cities, states, provinces and counties within three countries, the United States, Canada and Great Britain. It is a diverse and eclectic sampling of writings by women and men for whom sobriety within the fellowship of AA had nothing at all to do with an interventionist God.

"Don't Tell is an important book for anyone interested in the future of Alcoholics Anonymous and the future of alcoholism recovery." (From the Foreword by Ernest Kurtz, Author of *Not-God: A History of Alcoholics Anonymous*, and William White, Author of *Slaying the Dragon: The History of Addiction Treatment and Recovery in America.*) (Amazon)

––––––––

A Freethinker in Alcoholics Anonymous – John Lauritsen. (Published by Pagan Press on June 1, 2014.)

A Freethinker in Alcoholics Anonymous is written by an AA member with 46 years of continuous sobriety, who believes that he owes his life to the AA Fellowship. There are plenty of books that attack Alcoholics Anonymous or defend it uncritically or supplement it with personal testimonies or various tweaks. *A Freethinker in Alcoholics Anonymous* will be the first one to celebrate and defend the things in AA that are right, but also, with no holds barred, to criticize the things that are wrong and ought to be changed. An atheist for all of his adult life and a long-time contributor to the secular humanist press, Lauritsen bases his recovery on what he calls the True AA, the AA that works: the 24-Hour Plan and the Fellowship. He regards the religiosity in AA as detrimental to recovery from alcoholism. (Amazon)

––––––––

Common Sense Recovery: An Atheist's Guide to Alcoholics Anonymous – Adam N. (Second Edition published by AA Agnostica on January 5, 2015.)

The essays in this book explore in depth the confrontation of AA's religious culture and practices with this rational atheist alcoholic. They explore the place of science in recovery, and explain why traditional AA struggles to embrace new scientific findings and incorporate them into its agenda. The supreme importance of the fellowship, as a healing community or tribe, with all that implies for social human beings, is examined. Powerful arguments are presented for the idea that a secular AA would not lose any of its present efficacy, but could be even more effective, maybe much more effective, and would certainly help those alcoholics now repelled by religion. Adam has quite remarkably in this book woven a practical and viable way forward for AA. *Common Sense Recovery* offers an understanding and appreciation of AA's early religious culture that nevertheless and inevitably calls upon us to embrace new research and scientific findings – as well as the experience of women and men in recovery over the past 75 years – and incorporate them into an understanding of our program and fellowship. (Recovery 101)

––––––––

Do Tell! Stories by Atheists and Agnostics in AA – Roger C. (Published by AA Agnostica on May 12, 2015).

Our dear friend, the late Ernie Kurtz, said that storytelling is in fact "the practice and indeed the essential dynamic of AA". It is the way we AA members support each other and help guarantee our ongoing recovery. The stories in this book are all by AA members who do not believe that an interventionist deity – a God – had anything at all to do with their recovery from alcoholism. As readers will discover, many struggled mightily "in the rooms" with the idea of God or a Higher Power, wanting to fit in, as Alcoholics Anonymous was their last hope. There are a total of thirty stories in *Do Tell!* And they are very personal and honest stories. All unique, all different. The stories in the book alternate between those by women and those by men and so we discover – if we did not appreciate this already – that the factors involved in addiction and recovery are often quite different in the lives of men and women. As Marya Hornbacher says in the Foreword: *Do Tell!* is a "diverse and richly textured collection of recovery stories by non-believers... It is a book that would certainly have made a difference in the early days of my stumble toward sobriety and the Twelve Steps... It is also making a difference in my sobriety today." Enjoy these wonderful stories of "experience, strength and hope" by atheists and agnostics in AA. (Recovery 101)

––––––––

We also need to acknowledge two pieces of agnostic-friendly "Conference-approved" literature. The first is the book *Living Sober*, published in 1975. The second is the pamphlet "Do you think you are different?" which was published in 1976. It contains two stories by secularists: "My name is Ed, and I am an alcoholic (atheist)" and "My name is Jan, and I am an alcoholic (agnostic)".

Both of these were written and put together by a gay man by the name of Barry Leach, a staff writer for Alcoholics Anonymous. John Lauritsen, the author of *A Freethinker in AA*, describes *Living Sober* as "explicitly secular" and "independent from" religion. (**AA Beyond Belief**[5])

Articles about, by and for non-believers in AA have also been published by the AA Grapevine. A monthly magazine since June of 1944, the Grapevine has published just a little better than one article by a nonbeliever every two years. That is not entirely the Grapevine's fault: no doubt not a large number of articles by agnostics and atheists in AA have been submitted over the years.

However, in October 2016, the Grapevine devoted an issue to we agnostics in AA, called "Atheist & Agnostic Members". And at the April General Service Conference, it was agreed that the Grapevine would collect its already published forty or fifty articles by atheists and agnostics and publish them in a book. This would follow the same principle that resulted in a book published in 2014, *Sober & Out: Lesbian, Gay, Bisexual and Transgender AA Members Share Their Experience, Strength and Hope*, which contains 57 stories which had been published in the Grapevine between 1975 and 2011.

The October issue of the AA Grapevine was very well received. And we very much look forward to the book that contains the stories, the experience, strength and hope, of atheists and agnostics in AA.

This may not be perfection, but it is certainly progress.

Credit where credit is due.

We conclude this chapter on AA literature for we agnostics now, rather arbitrarily, with the Foreword I was pleased to write for the second edition of *The Alternative 12 Steps: A Secular Guide to Recovery*. This is shared out of respect and appreciation for the two authors of the book and also because it provides a kind of summary of and a positive closing to this particular chapter about literature for we agnostics in AA.

Here it is:

> *We can learn the universal, generic pattern of life's dance from the 12 Steps. But in our individual dance of life, we choose our own music and dance our own dance.*

> *Chapter on Step 3*

This is a remarkable book.

And there are at least two very good reasons for that.

Secular Steps

First, there is in this book, to the best of our knowledge, the first "non-Godly" version of the 12 Steps ever published.

The original version, of course, written by Bill Wilson and published in *Alcoholics Anonymous* in 1939, refers to God (or a "Power" or "Him") six times.

That's way too much God for many of us.

And, to be sure, many in AA had already taken action to circumvent the "God bit". In fact the term "God bit" comes from Jim Burwell, one of the first members of AA, who convinced Wilson to make the 12 Steps a "suggested" program of recovery – rather than a required one – in the AA fellowship.

Meetings for non-believers in AA have been around for a long time. Quad A (Alcoholics Anonymous for Atheists and Agnostics) was launched in 1975 in Chicago. Only a few years later, in Los Angeles, Charlie P and Megan D started the very first AA meeting called "We Agnostics". It is named, of course, after a chapter in *Alcoholics Anonymous* (often called the Big Book).

Today there are hundreds of AA meetings for agnostics and atheists in major cities across the United States and Canada. And more coming, more and more quickly.

Moreover, there is now plenty of literature for those who do not believe that an interventionist deity has a role to play in their sobriety.

For example, in 2013, Joe C published a book of daily reflections called *Beyond Belief: Agnostic Musings for 12 Step Life*. That same year *The Little Book: A Collection of Alternative 12 Steps* was published and it contains the secular version of the Steps, written by Martha Cleveland and Arlys G, which are at the core of this book.

All of the above is meant to place *The Alternative 12 Steps: A Secular Guide to Recovery* – written in the middle of this history in 1991 – in a historical context.

The "God bit" is hardly dealt with at all in this book, except in the intro-duction, as an impediment for many people who could otherwise do a 12-Step program. What the authors do is find the root power of each step, and reword it.

> *As 12-Step practitioners, we believe in the 12-Step program. We believe it can work for anyone. Our*

objective is to help non-religious people accept the healing power of the Steps. This is the same program, same principles, same values, same scope, same depth – all of it said in a little different language. We have extracted the actions and principles of the original Steps and put them into a secular context.

And they do it well! Anybody can understand Martha and Arlys. To use the Steps, there is no need for any particular religiosity; nor is there any need for psycho-jargon.

An example.

The original Step 6 says: "Were entirely ready to have God remove our defects of character."

Martha and Arlys reword that Step to say: "Be entirely ready to acknowledge our abiding strength and release our personal shortcomings."

In both cases, the person doing the Steps must be "entirely ready." But in this book, the work isn't relegated to God. It is up to the individual to be prepared to take action. And, in this version, the individual doesn't only deal with personal shortcomings (or "defects of character"), but also acknowledges an "abiding strength".

We shall deal with this more positive approach further on.

But in the meantime, we want to point out that, in fact, these can be the 12 Steps for anyone. Especially those without a belief in an interventionist God.

Women and the 12 Steps

The original 12 Steps were written by men for men. In particular, they were written for white men with well-to-do backgrounds.

This version of the Steps was written by two women.

Does that mean it is just for women?

No. It means that Martha and Arlys add some much needed balance to the Steps.

For instance.

There is a tremendous emphasis on "powerlessness" and "humility" in the original 12 Steps. While the idea of being powerless over alcohol makes sense, the idea that a human being is by his or her very nature powerless is another matter entirely. And yet it is deeply ingrained in the original Steps.

In this day and age, preaching powerlessness and humility to women would seem a bit off kilter.

But remember, the original Steps weren't written today or for women.

And, to come back to the religion part, they were deeply influenced by the religion of the day. The evangelical pietism of the Oxford Group, in which AA – and the Steps – had its origins, considered humans worthless. It emphasized a "deep aversion to all emphasis on human strengths." (*Not-God*, p. 180). You had to "Let go and let God." This attitude is very much embedded in the original 12 Steps.

And so when Martha and Arlys talk about acknowledging our "abiding strength," as they do in their version of Step 6, they are, if you will, "letting go of God", and recognizing that we human beings are indeed not powerless and have a part to play in our own sobriety, our most precious recovery.

And that is an important part of their version of the 12 Steps.

And it adds more balance between accepting the things we cannot change and mustering the courage to change what can and must be changed in our lives.

We are not criticizing the original 12 Steps or their author. Nor do Arlys and Martha do that in *The Alternative 12 Steps: A Secular Guide to Recovery*. Indeed, Bill Wilson never claimed to have written the perfect Steps. On the last page of the main part of the book *Alcoholics Anonymous* he wrote: "Our book is meant to be suggestive only. We realize we know only a little."

And this particular book is meant only to be a helping hand to we alcoholics who do not have a belief in a God and must inevitably "choose our own music and dance our own dance" on this generic but ultimately unique 12 Step road to recovery.

Let the story begin.

[1] **Barefoot's World**:
http://www.barefootsworld.net/aa24hoursbook.html

[2] **Recovery without Religiosity**:
http://paganpressbooks.com/jpl/ALK-FREE.HTM

[3] **A Proposal to Eliminate the Lord's Prayer from AA Meetings**:
http://aaagnostica.org/2011/11/17/a-proposal-to-eliminate-the-lords-prayer-from-aa-meetings/

[4] **Recovery 101**: http://recovery101.ca/

[5] **AA Beyond Belief**:
http://www.aabeyondbelief.com/2017/01/15/living-sober-the-book/

Chapter 13:
Santa Monica Convention

Word about a plan to hold a first international convention for agnostics, atheists and freethinkers in AA began to circulate in early April 2013.

The plan had originated with two alcoholic women, Dorothy H and Pam W, both members of We Agnostics, the meeting started in Hollywood in 1980 by Charlie Polacheck and Megan D.

They had discussed the idea of the convention between themselves rather cautiously over the month of January. But then, having discovered the AA Agnostica and Agnostic AA NYC websites, they realized that they were not alone, and that agnostic groups didn't only exist in Los Angeles. And then, reaching out to people like Deirdre S, the manager of the New York website, they discovered there was both support and enthusiasm for such a convention.

Dorothy, whose sobriety date is March 27, 2011, sent out an email to as many people as she could find on April 16, 2013. It contained a flyer about a We Agnostics / Free Thinkers International Alcoholics Anonymous Convention (WAFT IAAC) to be held in November 2014.

"Be of Service. Be a part of history." That's how it began.

And then it had several points including the following:

> • *Many of us struggled with religion and faith or know others who relapsed or left the rooms because they couldn't live the lie of belief. In this convention we want to address the struggles that each of us faces as we find our way in recovery and service work.*

> • *Our goal is to ensure that We Agnostics, non believers, and people who think god and religion is an outside issue know that they have a place within AA.*

> • *There are 22 states and 4 countries that have We Agnostic type meetings. Our goal is to bring us all together to discuss OUR experience, OUR strength, and OUR hope and to share solutions as free thinkers within the AA program.*

And then it ended with "Be of Service. Be a part of history. What you do can change things. We need your help."

A convention planning meeting was held on June 8, 2013. It brought together a small group of Californians and two people from Maui, Hawaii, Rich H and Joan C.

And the first official announcement came on June 16 when an article was published on AA Agnostica: **An AA Convention for We Agnostics**[1].

It featured an interview with Pam W and some of the details of the convention were shared. It would be held in Santa Monica, California, from Thursday to Saturday, November 6 through 8, 2014 at a Unitarian Universalist Church. Here's Pam:

> *We found a lovely location at the Unitarian Universalist Community Church in the center of Santa Monica, only a couple of miles from the beach. It has a courtyard with a BBQ and enough classrooms for several workshops and marathon meetings. The UU community is very embracing of non-believers and it has a special place in our history as the location of Chicago's Quad A's first meeting in 1975. It is a perfect place for this historic event.*

The convention would consist of panels, workshops and speakers, the details of which were still being worked out. There was also a plan to have back-to-back marathon-style meetings in a dedicated room. Agnostic groups from around the world would host these meetings with their own formats and agendas, allowing delegates at the convention to "travel" to meetings in New York, Chicago, Toronto, London, etc., without having to leave the room. Pam thought it would be helpful and "fulfilling to experience other non-religious styled meetings and share our different paths to recovery".

And the panels, workshops, speakers and meetings would all be part of the theme of the convention: "Many paths to recovery".

While there were regular planning meetings for the convention, most of the convention work was in the hands of a three person Steering Committee, consisting of Dorothy, Pamela and Jonathon Goley, another person who regularly attended the We Agnostics meeting in Hollywood. (Jonathan was found dead on October 18, 2014, less than one month before the convention.)

And the most active of those was certainly Dorothy.

In July and August 2013 she did a tour, visiting agnostic AA meetings in New York, Toronto and Chicago, successfully generating interest and enthusiasm.

As it turns out, speakers would be an important and inspiring part of the convention. There would be two types of speakers: "Keynote Speakers" and "Fellowship Speakers".

And why did people attend this first-ever convention for we agnostics? Let's hear from them. Here are reasons given by several people, all of which is excerpted from an article by Dorothy, **Convention Fellowship Speakers**[2], published on AA Agnostica on October 19, 2014.

Convention Fellowship Speakers

by Dorothy H

The convention registration so far represents how we agnostics and freethinkers in AA span the globe, with people from Canada, U.S., Philippines, Costa Rica, England, Spain, France, Ireland, Australia and American Samoa.

Our fellowship speakers have labored in love and anonymity for decades. Some are founders of meetings, prison panel leaders, authors, GSRs, webmasters, and founders of Internet groups and have dedicated years to WAFTs in AA. They gave countless hours of volunteer work to guarantee that our convention in November will be an amazing historical event...

Each speaker's contribution to AA is distinct and their stories follow.

Deirdre S

Deirdre S's service work is one of the pivotal reasons that people like me were able to get sober and stay sober. Deirdre's website, **Agnostic AA NYC**[3], with the World Agnostics AA Meeting List, would lead me to my homegroup, We Agnostics of Hollywood, CA.

The world list taught me WAFTs exist internationally. Deirdre was the first person I contacted about the convention. Deirdre responded to me by email on 3/31/13, she wrote: "I strongly believe that the goal of any discussion must be about staying IN AA and not trying to form a second organization and it looks like that's part of the agenda".

I addressed Deirdre's concerns that we were not a split! Once that was clear, Deirdre sent an email to her contact list to announce that we "were thinking of creating a convention". My inbox and voice mail was full of messages from people across the country and Canada pleading with us to move forward. Deirdre's response was the turning point that told Pam W and me that WAFT IAAC was possible and the Fellowship wanted it!

When I asked Deirdre why she thought the convention was important to her, she wrote:

> I don't have a lot of faith. What I have is experience. For the past 17 1/2 years it has been my experience that within the unstructured structure of Alcoholics Anonymous I have found a new way to live. I was never able to make my numerous decisions to stop drinking or cut down stick. I began finding my place in AA. This is something that didn't happen in my first six months of sobriety. I had to walk into an agnostic meeting before I met people who I really identified with unreservedly. There I could be completely honest. There I found real friendship and help. We each need to find our place and that is why coming to the first-ever conference for agnostics, free thinkers, and others was a must.

We all need to find our place, and Deirdre has been a pivotal resource for people within AA.

Joan C

This movement in AA is growing.

The first step of outreach work was to call people from the World AA Agnostic list. I called Maui, HI, and spoke to Rich H. Rich is one of the co-founders of three agnostic groups on Maui. After a three-hour talk, Rich called Joan C. She was his co-founder of the Maui groups.

Joan, as an old-timer, had left AA a few decades before. She felt her voice wasn't respected and that AA did not want her sober experience. When Rich approached her, it changed her life and the face of Maui AA. Joan did not stop at forming three meetings. She also started an independent women's prison panel. She continues to be of service to her local central office and has been a part of countless committees.

When I asked Joan why she thought the convention was important she said:

> *This convention is very important to me. It is something that I, in my forty-five years of sobriety, didn't think I would ever see. It confirms that we agnostics and free thinkers in AA are numerous enough to reassure the non-believing newcomer that he is in the right place for recovery. This movement in AA is growing and will continue to grow as more and more We Agnostics meetings are formed.*

Tim M

Tim spent his early sobriety in San Diego, CA. Tim comes from a Catholic family and has a wonderful relationship with his brother who is a Jesuit priest. He has been a cornerstone for the We Agnostics meeting in Los Feliz, CA, for over twenty years.

In shares, Tim describes his alcoholism as a desire not to feel.

When I asked Tim why he thought the convention was important he wrote:

> *What I am is a skeptic and non-believer; a philosophical perspective developed both honestly and independently of other important currents in my life, including alcoholism and recovery. What I am not is a proselytizer for atheism or any other creed. I respect the right of others to believe as they will. I contend that belief or non-belief is a matter of individual conviction and conscience. I believe that the point of the Convention is to assert that right of honest conviction and conscience with respect to belief or non-belief, to do so on behalf of every individual in the fellowship, and to insist that it be respected by all. Nothing less, nothing more.*

Respect for all is our goal. The Fellowship Speakers have been an inspiration to everyone in the WAFT world through their love and service! And they continue to give of themselves to make AA a place where we ALL can live honest and open lives.

We are a part of AA. And AA needs to be more inclusive. Those would be the central themes of the convention.

There would be great panels. There would be great workshops. All of the workshops and panels were held on the last two days – Friday and Saturday – of the Convention. A rough count indicates that there were some fifteen panels and twenty-one workshops. And there would be some thirty agnostic AA meetings held one after another throughout the last two days of the Convention.

Many of these are reported on AA Agnostica, which posted articles online at the end of each day of the Convention. You can read those here: **We Agnostics and Atheists AA Convention: Day 1, Day 2 and Day 3**[4,5,6]. And a fourth article recording events at the convention was posted ten days later: **Workshops at the WAFT Convention**[7].

Let us conclude this chapter with reports on the three rather exceptional keynote speakers at Santa Monica.

Marya Hornbacher, the author of several books including, *Waiting: A Nonbeliever's Higher Power*, ended the first day of the convention. Joe C, reporting on her talk, captured much of the mood of that first day of the first convention for non-believers in AA. First, he quotes Marya: "What I do have is the utmost faith in that I don't know... I don't get God but I do know awe and wonder and grace. I do know that I am grateful to be here and I do know that I am lucky to have found AA in you," referring to the agnostics, atheist and free thinkers listening to her with rapt attention.

Joe continues,

> I think that's how we all felt at the end of day of the first
> International meeting of nonbelievers in AA. We felt
> lucky, grateful to hear a day of speakers from the UK,
> France, Canada, Hawaii, New York, Chicago and from
> the host-state, California... It was nice to be part of AA
> history for a change. It would not surprise me that... by
> the 100th anniversary of AA, this historical day will be
> remembered as a meaningful turning point in AA. Many
> of the two to three hundred that gathered felt this
> modest shift in the direction in AA's future. Marya's talk
> expressed this hope that AA is and will progress.

Phyllis Halliday, the General Manager of the AA General Service Board, ended the second day of the Convention and Thomas B described her talk as "one of the major highlights of this week's magnificent milestone event".

And finally the last keynote speaker was Reverend Ward Ewing, a former Class A (non-alcoholic) Trustee and Chairman of the General Service Board of AA.

By the last day of the convention, attendance had grown to almost three hundred women and men. And, besides more engaging workshops, panels and marathon meetings, the rooms at the Unitarian Universalist Church in Santa Monica, California, were buzzing in anticipation of the closing talk to be delivered by Reverend Ward Ewing, who had been present throughout the Convention.

And as reported by Russ H: his talk was delivered "to a standing room only crowd of AA members". Russ continued: "Ward stands with us in our efforts to gain full and equal footing with AA. His vision clearly aligns with our own that... our secular membership and meetings of AA will inevitably take our place along all of the other mainstream facets of the AA fellowship. More importantly, he emphasized, is that this must happen."

Russ reported that Ward's talk concluded that for those who think that is impossible, well, as Ward "eloquently reminded us, AA is a place where the impossible becomes possible".

It was a great talk and ended the convention with a standing ovation.

[1] **An AA Convention for We Agnostics**:
http://aaagnostica.org/2013/06/16/an-aa-convention-for-we-agnostics/

[2] **Convention Fellowship Speakers**:
http://aaagnostica.org/2014/10/19/convention-fellowship-speakers/

[3] **Agnostic AA NYC**: http://www.agnosticaanyc.org/index.html

[4] **We Agnostics and Atheists AA Convention – Day 1**:
http://aaagnostica.org/2014/11/07/we-agnostics-and-atheists-aa-convention-day-1/

[5] **We Agnostics and Atheists AA Convention – Day 2**:
http://aaagnostica.org/2014/11/08/we-agnostics-and-atheists-aa-convention-day-2/

[6] **We Agnostics and Atheists AA Convention – Day 3**:
http://aaagnostica.org/2014/11/09/we-agnostics-and-atheists-aa-convention-day-3/

[7] **Workshops at the WAFT Convention**:
http://aaagnostica.org/2014/11/19/workshops-at-the-waft-convention/

Chapter 14:
Progress not Perfection

There were, however, controversies that emerged in the preparation for the Santa Monica, and the next, convention.

For this convention, the problem was sometimes trying too hard to be acceptable to all in AA. To conform, as it were, to conventional AA.

One of those controversies erupted in early 2014 when the Steering Committee decided to ban non-Conference-approved literature at the convention.

The WAFT IAAC website, created to provide information about the convention and to allow people to register and pay to attend, had a Frequently Asked Questions (FAQ) section. And one day in early 2014 in that section was this question, "Will there be non-Conference-approved literature at the convention?" followed by this answer: "Because we are a part of AA… the steering committee (SC) has decided not to allow any non-Conference-approved literature at the convention."

War broke out between the AA Agnostica side of the secular AA world and the convention Steering Committee.

And the Steering Committee went back and forth on the question, first saying there would be no non-Conference-approved literature, then saying the question was under consideration, then no again, and, after more objections, they replaced the "no" with a dash after the question "Will there be non-Conference-approved literature at the convention?" Presumably the dash meant either "we're thinking about it" or "we're avoiding dealing with it". Finally, after a couple of weeks of hemming and hawing the Steering Committee conceded and said it would "make this (non-Conference-approved) literature available in a separate, clearly defined location".

Why the debate at all? Why was there all the reluctance to include literature that hasn't been published by the AAWS? Even the General Service Office acknowledges that the term Conference-approved "does not imply Conference disapproval of other material about AA. A great deal of literature helpful to alcoholics is published by others, and AA does not try to tell any individual member what he or she may or may not read".

In the original FAQ on this subject, the Steering Committee said "Because we are a part of AA..." and then went on to "not allow" non-Conference-approved AA at the convention. The Committee was succumbing and conforming – knowingly or unknowingly – to the fundamentalists' vision of AA.

The second controversy was very much related. It was the selection of keynote speakers.

The first one we learned about was Marya Hornbacher, the author of several books including *Waiting: A Nonbeliever's Higher Power*. It's an excellent book and Marya turned out to be a wonderful speaker, and she spent all three days at the convention, also participating in a rather engaging panel called "Is Spirituality Compatible with Agnostic AA?"

But some – and not just a few – objected to Marya because she used her last name, and did not remain anonymous in line with Traditions Eleven and Twelve.

Two comments on that.

First, a number of writers are not anonymous, partly because it's hard to combine the two, writing and anonymity. Two examples: Ernest Kurtz, the author of *Not-God: A History of Alcoholics Anonymous*, and Dr. Allen Berger, the author of several books published by Hazelden, including *12 Stupid Things That Mess Up Recovery*.

These are authors. And their work has been enormously helpful to many of us in recovery. It is hard, if not impossible, to be an author and to remain anonymous, especially when writing about alcoholism and addiction.

Second, the Traditions are just that: Traditions. They are not Rules.

You also have to wonder just how relevant "anonymity" is today. We live in a different world, with the Internet and social media, and along with that the public acknowledgement and acceptance that many of us are afflicted with a variety of diseases, including addiction.

Is it the best thing to be "ashamed" of our alcoholism, and to try to hide it from others, to be "anonymous"? An organization founded in 2001, **Faces and Voices of Recovery**[1], thinks not. It advocates for better funding, research and legislation for alcoholics and addicts and suggests that part of achieving those goals is for those with long-term recovery to: "Stand up, stand out, speak out, and be proud about it. Of course, in early recovery, many seek the comfort and cocoon of anonymity. Eventually, it would be great to let everyone see the butterflies. We are many and we are beautiful."

That's certainly a different approach to helping ourselves and others to sustain our recovery.

But back to the speakers.

The other two keynote speakers would turn out to be Phyllis Halliday, at the time the General Manager of the General Service Office and the other one was Reverend Ward Ewing, a former Class A (non-alcoholic) Trustee and Chairman of the General Service Board of AA.

Clearly both speakers were selected to emphasize the link between our secular movement within AA and AA itself.

There is nothing wrong with that. It is laudable. And the Steering Committee certainly deserves credit for acknowledging and respecting that link.

But the crux of the problem was the "Reverend" part. There were rather vehement objections to someone with a belief in God – and whose profession was to share that belief – as a speaker at a convention for atheists, agnostics and freethinkers.

In an effort to deal with the problem, an article by Joe C was posted on AA Agnostica, **A Reverend at the Agnostic AA Convention**[2]. In it, Joe asks the question: "So, should a non-alcoholic, ordained minister speak at an AA convention for atheists and agnostics?" And ultimately his conclusion was: "I think it's great that the committee asked Ward Ewing. I think it's exciting that he agreed. Time will tell but my gut-instinct is that we will find a friend in the Reverend Ward Ewing."

Nevertheless, it was a problem that would persist, and related disputes would break out shortly after Santa Monica.

On the first day of the Santa Monica convention, a new WAAFT (We Agnostics, Atheists and Free Thinkers) IAAC (International Alcoholics Anonymous Convention) Board was elected with its mission being to organize the next convention for agnostics, atheists and freethinkers in AA. Also at that meeting, Austin, Texas, was selected as the location for the second international convention, to be held in 2016.

Dorothy, who had been re-elected as the Chair of the new Board, was targeted from the beginning. As John S, who worked with both Dorothy and the Board at the time, noted: "There was an organized plot to overthrow her, and the plotters ended up taking over the show".

In December of 2015, she submitted her resignation effective as of January 21, 2016. In her letter of resignation, she wrote:

> *I implore the board to literally reach out to the community when setting the tone and agenda for the convention. The tent should be big enough for everyone. If the convention is not as inclusive as possible, the WAAFT board will be behaving like those in AA we take considerable issue with.*

And she nailed what was precisely the Board's problem, at least at first: a not very inclusive approach. After Dorothy's resignation and the addition of new members including a new Chair, only four of the initial eleven people elected in Santa Monica remained on the Board.

And there was a Program Committee with its very own, and peculiar, agenda. As noted in an article on AA Agnostica in April of 2016, **The Second Secular AA Convention**[3], the first article published about a convention only a few months away:

> *Two members of the Program Committee, John C and John H, are apparently at least as extreme as Big Book Thumpers but on the opposite end of the spectrum: they are atheism thumpers. John H is aggressively opposed to any mention of the 12 Steps, secular or otherwise, and is contemptuous of words like "agnostic" or "spiritual".*

At a panel called "Afternoon with the Atheists" in the first hours of the first day of the Austin Convention, John H read the above quote. And then he said: "Guilty as charged". He then went on to trash views not in line with his own, referring, for example, to secular 12 Steps as a "watered down version of the fucking Apostle's Creed".

As a member of that audience put it, people in AA need to:

> *focus on what they do, not what they don't do and don't think anyone else needs to do either. If you don't do the steps, tell us what you DO do instead of bashing the steps. If you don't use a higher power, tell us what you do without bashing the higher power. Our primary purpose is to stay sober and help other alcoholics. (This talk was) an agenda that went beyond that. I found it very off-putting.*

Others would also later report that this first panel, and particu...
John H rants, set a negative tone for the convention. Indeed...
woman stopped going to AA meetings of any kind after Austin as s...
felt "very disenchanted after the conference".

There were, it should be acknowledged, other problems with the Austin convention.

One of them had to do with speakers, or the lack thereof. While the convention had three "Fellowship Speakers", and all three of them spoke on the first night, it had no "Keynote Speakers".

And that was a problem.

You see, listening to fellowship speakers, people like ourselves, in this case atheists and agnostics in AA, is a lot like talking to ourselves. Talking in a mirror. Sure, you understand and respect the views expressed. Sure you agree with them. But, anything new? Rarely.

What you should get from a keynote speaker, if she or he has been well chosen, is a larger perspective, a bigger picture. An under-standing of how your views fit in the grander scheme of things. These are talks that are thankfully "out of the box". They should be talks that are both illuminating and a genuine source of inspiration.

That's why there are speakers at conventions.

But the Board would have none of that.

The only proposed "keynote speaker" for this convention was Ami Brophy, the Executive Editor and Publisher of the AA Grapevine. The proposal resulted in chaos. She was considered an outsider... The Grapevine had far too many religious articles... A member of the Board, John C, threatened to organize demonstrations outside the entrance to the convention if she were to speak.

The Board yielded to him, and to not including any "keynote" speakers at the Convention.

In an article posted on AA Beyond Belief shortly after the convention, **Thinking About Austin**[4], John S wrote:

> I will say that I think the organizers of the convention
> dropped the ball by not giving Ami a full hour to speak
> to the entire convention on her own. I mean, she is the
> Executive Editor Publisher! It's a big deal. She speaks
> at the General Service Conference. There was a lot that
> we could have learned from her. If you had read her

keynote speakers was clearly one of the failings of
convention.

But let's stop there. Let's now talk about its successes. Because in the end it was a successful convention.

Like the Santa Monica convention, the Austin convention had a large variety of panels, workshops and meetings. It had over a dozen panels, ranging in topics from secular literature in AA (with Ami Brophy from the AA Grapevine as a panelist) to our movement's relationship to "conventional" AA. It had workshops on everything from "stoicism" to "meditation and recovery" to "the history of atheists and agnostics in AA". It had over twenty marathon AA meetings, organized and chaired by agnostic groups from around the world.

And, most importantly, it had an attendance of some 400 alcoholic men and women who shared, in a way that is only possible at an international convention of this sort, the "you are not alone" experience. As John S put it, prior to the convention, "No matter what, people will have fun. It's really about getting together". He was absolutely correct.

Read on. In the next Chapter, life-j will describe the Austin Convention, as he experienced it.

[1] **Faces and Voices of Recovery**:
http://facesandvoicesofrecovery.org/

[2] **A Reverend at the Agnostic AA Convention**:
http://aaagnostica.org/2014/04/13/a-reverend-at-the-agnostic-aa-convention/

[3] **The Second Secular AA Convention**:
http://aaagnostica.org/2016/04/17/the-second-secular-aa-convention/

[4] **Thinking About Austin**:
http://www.aabeyondbelief.com/2016/11/27/thinking-about-austin/

Chapter 15:
Austin Convention

by life-j

I missed out on the Santa Monica Convention, and I almost didn't make this one either, but the tooth fairy came through at the last moment.

And now I'm really stoked.

I had met a few of the people at a regional conference in Olympia, Washington, back at the beginning of the new year so I didn't feel entirely lost when I got to Austin. Even many years sober, occasions like this can be scary. Was I going to "fake it till you make it" and power through, or was I going to be a wall flower?

I started out with the former, as I was walking off to the Ethiopian restaurant down the freeway from the Crowne Plaza with a group of people I had just met, but I did manage to settle down after a fellow alcoholic asked me about it. Maybe it was too conspicuous. But after all, I was with my own kind here. In the end I came away with many good conversations with so many people that I'm having a hard time remembering who's who. You have to forgive me, I have brain damage.

But I will remember their faces two years from now in Toronto. I've never felt at home in a big crowd of people like I did here. And big it was, over 400 people registered for the convention, including people from several other countries, even as far away as Australia.

I'm not a suit and tie kind of guy, and I have felt out of place in hotels like this in the past, but even the hotel staff was pleasant and helpful and not judgmental. Maybe they had been warned by all the good people that put this together, that this might be an unusual bunch. Or am I just getting to be and act and feel normal, and haven't figured it out myself yet? Wouldn't be the first time I'm the last to see when I've changed.

I owe all of it to this program. God or no god, AA is where I learned how to live.

But on to the convention.

I'm amazed at how well it all came off. Thank you out-going board! There were many AA meetings, and I didn't manage to go to a single one – there were just too many interesting topic panels and workshops to go to, often more than one at a time: ranging all the way from hardcore atheist rants to the spiritual, talks on AA history, on the future of AA, on all the odd aspects of AA mythology, and inconsistencies in our literature, on legal matters, including the Ontario Human Rights Tribunal suit, and on our relations to medical and psychiatric problems, GLBTQ and other subgroups.

We had a banquet Friday night, and I sat down at a table with people I didn't know without feeling self conscious for even a minute. It probably didn't directly do much for my sobriety, but let me tell you, I have been to too many AA get-togethers with gross spaghetti dinners. This was absolutely fabulous. With the banquet we also had three speakers, and they were all good. It was especially good to hear the talk delivered by Deirdre S, from New York City.

Ami from the Grapevine was there, giving us feedback about how we can help the Grapevine help us. We are after all only one of the subgroups they have to look after, but with the October issue, "Atheist and Agnostic Members", it really feels like they do try to help us. We're finally seeing real signs of the service structure supporting us as real members of AA.

One topic I heard brought up several times was why we're not simply making our own program entirely. But we're all aware that AA got us sober, AA is where we belong, and it's where we have an obligation to the newcomer unbeliever so they will not have to feel as alone as we often did before we found each other. AA is just too big an entity to abandon to the fundies.

I got to go to a local regular Austin AA meeting with a couple of other attendees, and of course there I heard several people say the same thing I've heard so many times: I'm really having trouble finding my higher power.

We're still needed out there to help them know that they do not need to!

As a convention we also looked forward to the next one in 2018. It was decided to hold it in Toronto, at the downtown Marriott hotel from August 24 to 26, and we also voted in a new board. There were a few tense moments, but I think we eventually wound up with a group of very talented and dedicated people. I was especially pleased to see at least one young person on the new board.

We also chose a new name for the next convention. WAAFT IAAC would still have served us, especially if we had just added a couple of more letters to the acronym, but eventually we arrived at the name, International Conference of Secular AA (ICSAA) instead. I like it. One thing which carried it was the thought that since a secular alternative to AA is being called for from several corners, we might as well begin calling ourselves secular.

Specific panels? It's kind of a blur, still. I got something good out of every one I went to. One that stands out to me was the Mental Health Issues and Recovery, where we had a couple of psychiatrists, both in the program, talk with us. Though Bill Wilson himself knew mental problems all too well to claim that AA could fix it, we have heard way too much about that from many recent members. It was good to have these two doctors here to talk with. I have a friend with severe mental issues who is very dear to my heart, and we need much more involvement with the professionals among us, rather than more step work, so we can help them instead of making them more desperate for supposedly not working that program right which, which we are so often falsely told, fixes absolutely everything if only it is done right.

Sunday night I went to dinner with a couple of other people. One of them I knew pretty well, one I had never really met before, and then there was Roger. I know you're a humble person, and would be inclined to strike this from the article, since I'm publishing this on your site. But you can't do that. As I'm sitting here in the airport on my way home writing this, this is so big, I'm sitting here and I'm beginning to cry. It's not something I do often. But I'm aware that none of all this would probably have happened if it wasn't for you. Granted, our secular movement has gotten me into a lot of trouble with local AA, but it has also given me a new life, a new group of people with whom I can relate with honesty.

And that new life was reinforced dramatically at the convention in Austin.

All too much to handle with a straight face. Tears are actually rolling now, I better stop here. Probably everyone sitting here around me thinks I'm flying away from bad romance behind me or something. On the contrary, I have a wonderful woman waiting for me at home, another gift of the program, since I don't have to be an asshole anymore. Life is good. Thank you. Thank you everyone.

I look forward to seeing you in Toronto in 2018.

Chapter 16:
A Growing Secular Movement

Riding the Tide

We are a rapidly growing and evolving secular movement within Alcoholics Anonymous.

Our "godfather", if you will, was Jim Burwell, back in the 1930s. That's where we all – I trust – learned the importance of "widening our gateway".

There were the first agnostic AA meetings in the 1970s and 80s in Chicago, Los Angeles and New York City thanks to men and women like Don Wilson, Charlie Polacheck, Megan D and Ada Halbreirch.

And then there is the explosion in this decade. It's a tide that promises to bring about a new era in Alcoholics Anonymous. And we didn't create this tide. That's not how a movement happens. It happens as a result of a real need suddenly experienced by a significant segment of a population: people who find it impossible to go forward without real change, a transformation that respects them and their needs. Ask the black or LGBTQ people. We are like surfers riding that tide. And our end goal is really quite simple. As an AA trustee put it in 1976, we non-believers need to know that we "are not merely deviants, but full, participating members in the AA Fellowship without qualification."

It's quite the tide within Alcoholics Anonymous.

And we are going to look at two ways in which this tide has grown and gained momentum within our Fellowship: websites and meetings.

———

AgnosticAANYC[1]

The first website we want to talk about is one in New York City, a website which actually came to be because of 9/11. September 11, 2001 fell on a Tuesday, the same day as the home group meeting of Deirdre S. Her meeting was cancelled as it turned out to be in a closed off part of the city. Trying to find people was a real problem. Deirdre shared the following at the Austin convention:

It was just after that that Charles P. floated the idea of having a website where NYC members could check and see if a meeting was happening or not. The website came to be in mid-2002. He also created some email lists at the same time. He carefully wrote a questionnaire about what people wanted and needed in a website and created it. The website started with a list of NYC meetings, Frequently Asked Questions, a national list of meetings put together by Leonard V. and others, and some meeting scripts and other documents.

Deirdre took over the site in 2006. A Website Committee was formed to get a group conscience of the New York City members as to what should appear of the website. It was then revised to be a "facts only" information resource after the issue of what to do about some more personal reflections that had been added to the website in an area called the "Member Zone" was opposed by one member. After the formation of the Website Committee, a report about the costs, content, and growth of the New York City and Worldwide meetings was to be issued once a year and distributed.

The expansion of the "national" list of meetings in 2002 had by then become an "international" list of meetings. This was enormously helpful over the years for anyone looking for a secular AA meeting. And it was a key component in deciding to hold the convention in 2014. After all, there were other agnostic AA meetings across the world. And there were people and groups that could be contacted and invited to participate at the convention.

After hearing about the proposed convention and meeting Dorothy H, on April 2, 2013, Deirdre did just that. She sent out a message to her contacts who for the very first time heard about "A call for an agnostic AA Conference coming out of California" (the subject of her email).

In the email, Deirdre quotes Dorothy, who is grateful to and relying upon the agnosticAANYC website: "There are 22 states and 4 countries that have We Agnostic type meetings. Our goal is to bring us all together to discuss OUR experience, OUR strength, and OUR hope and to share solutions as free thinkers within the AA program."

The website played a crucial role in providing essential contacts for this convention.

Let's back up just a bit to share that, over the years, the website was not without its own controversies and challenges.

One of the documents it had decided to include on the website was a secular version of the 12 Steps. This got the attention of the AA General Service Office.

On September 28, 2010, Gayle S R, a GSO staffer, wrote to the administrator of the Agnostic AA NYC website. In the letter Gayle points out that the website refers to "addicts" as well as alcoholics – still a no-no in at that time in "old school" AA. Worse, the secular version of the 12 Steps was available on the website.

"So we respectfully request that your group stop calling itself an AA group," Gayle concluded.

The "group" removed the modified 12 Steps, and any reference to addicts, from the website and that has not changed, to this very day.

Finally, on February 25, 2017, the agnosticAANYC website turned over the job of listing all international agnostic AA meetings to another AA website, "Secular AA" (more on this later). The website will remain but just for its New York City members and meetings. For fifteen years it had listed – and constantly updated – secular AA meetings across the world. For many years, this website was one of the only places for people to find answers to queries about meetings for agnostics, atheists, freethinkers and others. Much of the business of answering those questions was done by Charles P, Jason N, Sam M, and Mel D, all members from New York City.

"It's the end of an era for agnosticAANYC!" Deirdre wrote.

It certainly was. And Deirdre deserves a great deal of credit for the role she and the agnosticAANYC website played in that era.

AA Agnostica[2]

The website AA Agnostica was launched almost a decade after the New York City website, on June 15, 2011.

And at first it was called "AA Toronto Agnostics". It was created immediately after the expulsion of the two groups, Beyond Belief and We Agnostics, from the Greater Toronto Area Intergroup. David R, the long-time secretary of Beyond Belief, was sent out to purchase a domain name and launch a website, with the sole purpose of letting the newcomer to AA know the locations and times of the two groups' meetings.

In the first few weeks I took over from David as the site administrator. David was devastated by the booting out of his group and would leave AA, never to return.

And the website began to grow. At the time I was working on "A History of Agnostic Groups in AA" which I thought would be completed over a weekend or two but which took a full three months. And that project, and the need to share it online, led to the thought that the website could be more than simply a notice of agnostic AA meetings in Toronto.

On June 22, 2011, "Anarchy Melts", an article by Bill Wilson originally published by the AA Grapevine in July 1946, was posted on the website. It was thought to be entirely appropriate to begin with an article by the co-founder of Alcoholics Anonymous. On September 27, 2011, "A History of Agnostic Groups in AA" was finally published. Between the publications of these two, only five other articles were posted on the website.

Six months in, in early January, 2012, inspired to go fully international, AA Toronto Agnostics became AA Agnostica and adopted the motif: "A space for AA agnostics, atheists and freethinkers worldwide".

And it discovered it was surfing atop a ferocious tide.

On its first anniversary it was reported in the post **One Year Old!**[3] that, "To date, forty-six articles have been published on this website, and these have been written, remarkably, by twenty-two different people. These writers are from two continents (Europe and North America), and over a dozen cities (London, England and Toronto, Canada through to New York and Minneapolis and Austin and Los Angeles, United States)".

And that post goes on to report:

> There is lots of history here for the history buff. "AA in the 1930s: God as We Understood Him" is a good example. And there's a biography of the first atheist in Alcoholics Anonymous to make a difference in terms of the accessibility of AA to all with a desire to quit drinking: "Jim Burwell". Last year also saw the death of the very first person to use "We Agnostics" as the name of a group in AA. Charlie P had 41 years of continuous sobriety when he died in February of this year at the age of 98. "Father of We Agnostics Dies" tells the story of this remarkable man, for whom an AA meeting was

held at his bedside in the week before he died. (One Year Old!)

And so it would be for the next six years.

And for the record, AA Agnostica has never had a Board of or a Committee of any kind. In the early months I organized an ad hoc committee meeting, consisting of members from each of three agnostic groups in the Toronto area, to talk about the website. At that meeting, Dianne P, later to become the Chair of the Austin convention Board, rather surprisingly moved that a secular version of the 12 Steps be removed from AA Agnostica. Everyone voted in favour of her motion except her husband, John M.

The Steps were never removed. And as I left that meeting, I thought, "Well, that's it. That's the last Committee Meeting". And it was. It should also be noted, however, that if an article was in any way dubious or controversial, I would send it to three or four people to get their feedback as to whether or not it should be posted on AA Agnostica, and over the years that certainly proved to be helpful. So there was something of a "group conscience" for the website.

On its fourth anniversary (mid-June, 2015) it was reported that 94 articles had been published over the previous twelve months and this was in comparison to 62 the previous year and 46 in both years one and two of AA Agnostica. The 94 articles had been written by 50 different people and eight articles had been devoted directly to the We Agnostics, Atheists and Free Thinkers (WAAFT) convention in November in Santa Monica. (**Four Years Old!**[4])

And other projects had been undertaken by the website. From February 2 until November 15, 2014 AA Agnostica hosted a chatroom. This was managed by life-j and ended when he became ill for a prolonged period.

And more importantly, for three years, beginning in mid-March 2013 and ending on June 15, 2016, AA Agnostica helped nonbelievers start their own agnostic AA meetings. On the Home Page was a message that read, "Want an agnostic AA group in your town or city? Click here". And thousands of people did just that, and filled out a form with their location, email address, and an optional phone number and comment. If others nearby did the same, they would be connected, filled in on what needed to be done, and often a new meeting would be launched. This was all managed by Chris G who estimates that this project helped start approximately eighty meetings throughout

North America, at a time when people felt very uncomfortable doing just that. The situation is not nearly as bad today.

In September of 2015, AA Agnostica announced that, in the AA spirit of rotation, it would be turning over much of its work, in particular the regular Sunday posts, to another website, AA Beyond Belief, managed by John S. (More on this website later.) It would continue to help people start meetings and to post the occasional article, however, mostly on Wednesdays. And then on its fifth anniversary on June 15, 2016, having by then posted a total of 360 articles, AA Agnostica announced that it would cease posting any new articles. (**The Last Post**[5])

But it didn't. Why not?

The answer is simple and was mentioned earlier on: the wave we are on is just too ferocious. It's near impossible to jump off and put the board away. It's gratifying to be a part of letting the still suffering alco-holic – especially the one who does not believe in an interventionist deity – know that she or he is not alone in Alcoholics Anonymous. But we will stop. We'll publish this book and post it – one chapter at a time – on AA Agnostica. And come mid-June in 2017 we'll post an article, "**Six Years Old!**" to bring things up-to-date.

After that? Well. We'll see. One day at a time.

Rebellion Dogs Publishing[6]

This website, launched by the author of *Beyond Belief*, Joe C, posted its first blog on September 21, 2011 and that was about Joe's inter-view with Marya Hornbacher and her book, *Waiting: A Nonbeliever's Higher Power*.

Joe wanted a place where he could archive his musings about life in recovery.

As well as having a number of articles on the site, there are also audio recordings and podcasts. The first podcast dates back to the de-listing of Vancouver agnostic AA groups in late 2013.

Rebellion Dogs Publishing. Where does the name come from? In the mid-1980s Joe was in a band called Skid Row and it played a song by Cathy R called "Rebellion dogs our every step" and an actual scary dog was a metaphor in the song. Of course the sentence "Rebellion dogs our every step at first" is from page 73 of *Twelve Steps and Twelve Traditions*.

AA Beyond Belief[8]

It was indeed the spirit of rotation that brought abr
Belief.

It was in the summer of 2015 that John S and I began ᴜᴎᴄ
that would have the new website take over the commitment to pus.
articles by atheists and agnostics in AA each and every Sunday.

Why was John approached to do this work?

To begin with, it was clear that he understood the problems faced by
secularists within the Fellowship.

With a sobriety date of July 20, 1988, John had joined AA and for the
next decade he accepted the religiosity of AA. However, by 2011,
having read *The God Delusion* by Richard Dawkins and *God is Not
Great* by Christopher Hitchens, he knew that he was an atheist. What
to do? He found that it was impossible to be honest about that in
conventional AA. "It got to where I couldn't stand it any longer. I
started speaking honestly, and people at my home group didn't like it.
I felt that I was no longer accepted."

Does any of that sound familiar?

With a friend, Jim C – the only open atheist he knew in AA – John
launched the first ever agnostic group in Missouri, called We
Agnostics Kansas City. It held its first meeting on August 7, 2014. A
few months later, in November, he would attend the We Agnostics and
Freethinkers convention in Santa Monica. That is where we first met.
John also had a great deal of experience working on the Internet and
had launched a website for his home group on July 20, 2014, a few
weeks before its first meeting. As noted earlier on, he also became
the webmaster for WAAFT Central, launched on November 12th, just
after the convention.

So what would stop John from launching AA Beyond Belief and taking
over much of the role played until then by AA Agnostica? Nothing at
all. The first article on the website, by Roger C, was posted on
Sunday, October 4, 2015, and was called "Platitudes in AA".

AA Beyond Belief has grown impressively since its origins. It has a
Board of Directors responsible solely for the finances of the website. It
also has an Editorial Board, which includes Doris A, the chief editor,
as well as Galen T and Mary K. And it has three people who are
responsible for art and photography: Cope C, Jan A and Kathryn F. All
of these people are unpaid volunteers.

yond Belief also does podcasts, a role at which John excels. [ ] than 50 podcasts have been produced with 69,000 downloads [ ] people from across the globe. "In addition to personal stories, the podcast covers such topics as the Twelve Steps, the Twelve Traditions, AA service work, alternatives to AA, and news and announcements. Going forward, we hope to include interviews with authors in the recovery community, as well as professionals in the field of alcohol and drug addiction treatment." (**AA Beyond Belief**[9])

All podcasts are posted on YouTube and Sound Cloud. As well articles are now also in audio format, work done by Len R, and are also available on YouTube.

In less than a year and a half, AA Beyond Belief has achieved great goals and great successes. Articles are posted every Sunday, which express the diversity of our secular community within AA. They are about AA history, book reviews, current news as well as the experience, strength and hope of people who in other forums would be unable to be open and honest. And, for some, the podcasts have made Wednesday their favorite day of the week.

Doris and John describe the mission of AA Beyond Belief: "This is all about sharing our experience that recovery in Alcoholics Anonymous is open to anyone regardless of belief or lack of belief".

Mission accomplished.

———

Meetings

When I first began writing "A History of Agnostic Groups in AA" back in the summer of 2011, there were a grand total of 87 agnostic AA groups across North America. Today there are…

Well, let's go back and start at the beginning, or at least as the numbers were reported by Deirdre in her talk at the Austin convention. (**A History of Special Interest Groups in AA**[10])

Deirdre reports that when she came into the rooms in 1997, there were 26 agnostic-type meetings nation-wide. "As of September 23, 2001 there were 36 meetings nationally. In 2003 there were 38 meetings, in 2004, there were 57, in 2009 there were 71, in 2012 there were 99 meetings."

When Deirdre spoke at the 2014 conference in Santa Monica that number had grown to 181 agnostic AA meetings worldwide.

In the next year growth spiked to 288 meetings.

And when she spoke at the 2016 conference in Austin the number of "agnostic type" meetings, according to the agnosticAANYC website, had reached 320 meetings worldwide. As she correctly noted: "That number of meetings and people have real weight in AA. As we have seen by the gatherings at our conventions in Santa Monica and here today, those 320 meetings represent thousands of people and decades of sobriety. This is a material force that must be dealt with by AA." (A History of Special Interest Groups in AA)

The last number she provided was for November 11, 2016 and that was 320 secular meetings worldwide.

The last time I checked, there were 384 secular meetings worldwide, according to the folks who manage the Secular AA website. That's an increase due in small part to combining all of the lists but it is mostly the result of meetings that have been launched since the Austin convention.

That's impressive. Truly.

So let's talk a little about these secular meetings.

First, they are not clichéd in a way that is the case for many conventional AA meetings. You won't find the 12 Steps ("Power... God... God... God... Him... God... Him...") on a huge placard at the front of the room. How It Works from the Big Book will not be read at the beginning of the meeting. And it won't end with the Lord's Prayer.

A big difference already, right?

Here is what many of the meetings do have in common, however: There will probably be readings at the beginning of the meeting, and these could very well include the AA Preamble and/or the Agnostic AA Preamble. And many of the meetings for agnostics, atheists and free-thinkers end with the Responsibility Declaration.

That's it, that's all. And none of this is universal.

For instance, some meetings end with "Live and Let Live!" in the same way that the first meetings in 1986 at Ada's house in New York ended. And the way that the meeting she started – now called "We Humanists" and held at the Jan Hus Church – still ends to this day. Bob K reports that the Whitby Freethinkers (Ontario) end this way: "Closing the meeting is rather straightforward and without ritual – the chair simply thanks everyone and encourages attendance the following week".

At my We Agnostics meeting in Hamilton, as a result of group consensus, we start with four readings – a secular version of the 12 steps, the AA and the Agnostic AA preambles, and an edited version of Appendix II. I personally think that the readings help people to settle down, remind them that they are at a meeting for alcoholics and generally set the tone for a good meeting. We end with the Responsibility Declaration.

Formats for secular meetings also vary a great deal, but most of them provide an opportunity for those present to share in an honest way. Meetings can begin with a reading (usually from *Living Sober* or *Beyond Belief*) or a speaker who shares for ten or fifteen minutes. Another option is to choose and discuss two or three topics. All of this can change though, if there is a newcomer present. At our "topic" meeting in Hamilton, if there is a newcomer the first and most focussed upon topic automatically becomes Step 1 and Tradition 3.

Those are some options. But remember: there are no rules.

Are you an alcoholic? Is there an agnostic AA group nearby? If not, why don't you start one?

All it takes, we are told, is resentment towards the other meetings in your neighborhood and a coffeepot. You can get some more information on how easy it is here, **How to Start an AA Meeting**[11], on AA Agnostica, or here, **Start a Meeting**[12], on Secular AA.

Your meeting could be one of many agnostic AA meetings launched next month.

That's right: climb on top of this ferocious tide!

You will be doing yourself and others a favor by becoming a part of a wonderful and healthy movement within the Fellowship of Alcoholics Anonymous.

Ride the tide.

[1]**AgnosticAANYC**: http://agnosticaanyc.org/

[2]**AA Agnostica**: http://aaagnostica.org/

[3]**One Year Old!**: http://aaagnostica.org/2012/06/10/one-year-old/

[4]**Four Years Old!**: http://aaagnostica.org/2015/06/14/four-years-old/

[5]**The Last Post**: http://aaagnostica.org/2016/06/15/the-last-post/

[6]**Rebellion Dogs Publishing**:
https://www.rebelliondogspublishing.com/home

[7]**WAAFT Central / Secular AA**: https://www.secularaa.org/

[8]**AA Beyond Belief**: https://aabeyondbelief.org/

[9]**AA Beyond Belief**: https://aabeyondbelief.org/2017/03/05/aa-beyond-belief-the-thinking-persons-grapevine/

[10]**A History of Special Interest Groups in AA**:
http://aaagnostica.org/2016/12/15/a-history-of-special-interest-groups-in-aa/

[11]**How to Start an AA Meeting**: http://aaagnostica.org/how-to-start-an-aa-meeting/

[12]**Start a Meeting**: http://www.secularaa.org/start-a-meeting/

Conclusion:
Who We Are

One of the favorite quotes I came across in early recovery was the following: "It does me no injury for my neighbor to say there are twenty gods or no God. It neither picks my pocket nor breaks my leg." (Thomas Jefferson, *Notes on Virginia*, 1782)

Jefferson might well have added, "You can get sober with a God or without a God. So what?"

Exactly. No broken legs. No pockets picked.

This is a reality that conventional AA needs to come to understand. It has to stop insisting that a Higher Power – whom many choose to call God – is an essential part of recovery and sobriety. It has to stop suggesting that if you don't get that, you will get drunk.

Plain and simple. Or the future of AA is not good.

That has been put very gently.

My very favorite quote about AA is from Bill Wilson. It was part of a talk he gave to the 1965 General Service Conference in New York. After thirty years, Bill was now able to perfectly define and describe the fellowship he had co-created thirty years earlier. Here is that definition:

> In AA we are supposed to be bound together in the kinship of a universal suffering. Therefore the full liberty to practice any creed or principle or therapy should be a first consideration. Hence let us not pressure anyone with individual or even collective views. Let us instead accord to each other the respect that is due to every human being as he tries to make his way towards the light. Let us always try to be inclusive rather than exclusive. Let us remember that each alcoholic among us is a member of AA, so long as he or she so declares.

A kinship of a universal suffering.

The full liberty to practice any creed or principle or therapy.

Let us not pressure anyone with individual or even collective views.

t is due to every human being.

y to be inclusive rather than exclusive.

among us is a member of AA, so long as he or she so

So who are we alcoholic agnostics, atheists and freethinkers in the rooms? Well, the correct answer to that question is very simple:

We are members of AA.

As we so declare.

And many of us are inspired to work to help AA do what it must do in this twenty-first century. And that is to move forward, to drop some of the "very bad dogma" (Bill W) so often prevalent in the rooms of AA today. We shall do this work so that the hand of AA will always be there "when anyone anywhere reaches out for help".

For that we are all responsible.

Appendix I
Secular Versions of "How It Works"

A New "How It Works"

John S
We Agnostics Kansas City

Writing the book *Alcoholics Anonymous*, what we today call the Big Book, was a moment of genius and creativity. I can just imagine the excitement in the room when Bill read the steps to the group for the first time, and what an interesting debate it must have been as they hashed over the precise wording. There were those on one side who wanted the program to be religious, specifically Christian, and there were others who wanted it to be completely secular, no god at all, and those who were between the two camps who helped bring about a compromise.

Imagine the passion those early members felt for the fellowship as they watched it grow, as they made new friends while getting sober together!

New groups were forming all over the country and AA was a real movement that was really going somewhere. The fellowship was looking forward, to the future. It was free of any burden from the past, no founding fathers to revere, no sacred texts, everything was fresh. The Twelve Traditions formed from AA's early experience were form-ally adopted in 1950 when AA was only fifteen years old. The AA members of that time were experiencing a program that was designed by their generation and for their generation.

Sadly, this doesn't describe AA in the 21st Century.

No longer is AA looking forward to the future, instead it clings to the past. The AA of today is no longer dreaming, no longer tapping into the collective imagination and talents of its membership. AA isn't building anything new for future generations. In twenty-four years, the Big Book will be 100 years old! Those of us who are members of the fellowship today should be horrified at the thought that this book will be used as the central text in the year 2039.

That's not the future any of us should wish for AA.

It's time to get some movement back into this movement.

What could "How It Works" look like at an AA meeting in the 22nd century?

This is my effort to answer that question.

We are Alcoholics Anonymous, members of a world-wide fellowship of men and women united by a common purpose to stay sober and help others to recover from alcoholism. For us alcohol was cunning, baffling and powerful. It took us to that great jumping off place where we met terror, bewilderment, frustration and despair. Without help it was too much for us!

But we found help in Alcoholics Anonymous and the collective experience of those who preceded us in recovery. Here, we learned that honesty, open mindedness and willingness were indispensable if we were to reclaim our lives. Although our personal stories and experiences vary, this is a general description of the path we took.

We admitted we were powerless over alcohol – that our lives had become unmanageable. This humbling admission was a relief, the fight was over. We came to believe we could be helped through the fellowship of Alcoholics Anonymous, and we made a decision to turn away from obstinate denial, to let go of our old ways, and to follow suggestions.

We took stock of ourselves to uncover the truth about who we were and the events that shaped our lives, and we shared our stories in their entirety with another person, leaving nothing out. Through this process we learned the value of character building and we persistently worked to let go of those personal traits that blocked us from our usefulness to others. Understanding the damage left in the wake of our drinking, we made amends to those we had harmed, except when to do so would injure them or others.

Having followed these suggestions, our old ideas and attitudes were replaced with a new outlook on life. We became less interested in ourselves and more interested in the welfare of others. Our past became our greatest asset, the primary tool to help other alcoholics. At last, we felt that we were set on a new course.

We maintained this new attitude by continuing the practice of personal inventory and when we were wrong, promptly admitting it. We sought to improve our conscious awareness of these principles, and the serenity, courage and wisdom to carry them out. Everything we had done and all that we experienced to this point produced within us a deep and meaningful transformation, and having had this experience, we tried to carry this message to other alcoholics and to practice these principles in all our affairs.

This may seem a daunting task, but we assure you that none of us follow these principles perfectly, they are suggestions only, and there is no requirement they be followed at all. Together, we have recovered and with us so can you.

We members of Alcoholics Anonymous of the 21st Century need to build on the foundation that was laid by the AA of yesterday. The time has come to build something new, something better that will reach more people, save more lives and make a real difference. In order to do this, we need to stop clinging to the past. Honor it yes, even revere it, but we mustn't let it burden us. If we don't take responsibility for this fellowship and help to prepare it for the 22nd Century, then we are doing a grave disservice to the founders. Alcoholics Anonymous simply cannot survive long into the future if it refuses to dream, to change, to adapt and adopt, to think big.

We have the technology to gather the experience of millions of alcoholics the world-over and to transmit that experience in the language of our generation. We can and should rethink everything. For example, can't we have more than one version of the steps? Can't we take the principles of the steps and translate them into language for people of all faiths or people with no faith at all? If an AA group somewhere decides to write its own version of the steps while staying true to the basic tenets, isn't that something we should celebrate and encourage?

There's a lot of excitement among the agnostics, atheists and freethinkers in AA. We are writing new literature, blogs, creating websites, holding conventions, creating new groups, workshops for new groups, rethinking the steps, even debating these things. It's an exciting time, a time of change. This is where the change begins, but the rest of the fellowship needs to join in. We need to build it together or we will ultimately drift apart.

Change is coming, it's inevitable, but we have a duty and obligation to those who preceded us to act as capable stewards of the fellowship so that future generations can build on our work.

An Updated "How It Works"

Hilary J
Sober Agnostics Group, Vancouver, BC

The program is a tool to help us to recover from our addictions. It requires us to be completely honest with ourselves, and to take personal responsibility for our own behaviour and attitudes. We have found this to be a crucial element in our recovery.

Our stories disclose in a general way what we used to be like, what happened, and what we are like now. If you truly desire recovery, and are willing to go outside your comfort zone and work hard to change your life and your behaviour, then you are ready to take certain steps.

Some of these appeared very daunting. At first, most of us thought we could find an easier, softer way; but we could not. Half measures availed us nothing. We stood at the turning point, and chose the path to sobriety. Here are the Steps we took, which are suggested as a program of recovery:

1. We admitted we were powerless over our addictions - that our lives had become unmanageable.

2. Came to accept that we needed strengths beyond our awareness and resources to cope with our problems.

3. Made a decision to use the program to overcome our addiction.

4. Made a searching and fearless moral inventory of ourselves: acknowledging our strengths and weaknesses, and the fears, resentments and selfish behaviours that contributed to our addiction.

5. Admitted to ourselves without reservation, and to another human being, the details of that inventory, both positive and negative.

6. Were ready to let go of our destructive patterns.

7. Humbly sought to change our behaviour and attitudes in order to achieve sobriety.

8. Made a list of all persons we had harmed and became willing to make amends to them all.

9. Made direct amends to such people wherever possible, except when to do so would injure them or others.

10. Continued to take personal inventory, and when we were wrong promptly admitted it.

11. Searched within ourselves for our rightful path in life and the power to carry that out.

12. Having achieved recovery through taking these steps, we tried to carry this message to other addicts, and to practice these principles in all our affairs.

Many of us exclaimed, "What an order! I can't go through with it". Do not be discouraged. No one among us has been able to maintain anything like perfect adherence to these principles. We are not saints. The point is that we are willing to work hard to improve our lives and maintain our recovery. The principles we have set down are merely guides. We claim progress rather than perfection.

"How It Works"

Live and Let Live Group of Bloomington-Normal, Illinois

Rarely have we seen a person fail who has thoroughly followed our path. Those who do not recover are people who cannot or will not completely give themselves to this simple program, usually men and women who are constitutionally incapable of being honest with themselves. There are such unfortunates. They are not at fault; they seem to have been born that way. They are naturally incapable of grasping and developing a manner of living which demands rigorous honesty. Their chances are less than average. There are those, too, who suffer from grave emotional and mental disorders, but many of them do recover if they have the capacity to be honest.

Our stories disclose in a general way what we used to be like, what happened, and what we are like now. If you have decided you want what we have and are willing to go to any length to get it — then you are ready to take certain steps.

At some of these we balked. We thought we could find an easier, softer way. But we could not. With all the earnestness at our command we beg of you to be fearless and thoroughly from the very start. Some of us have tried to hold on to our old ideas and the result was nil until we let go absolutely.

Remember that we deal with alcohol — cunning, baffling, powerful! Without help it is too much for us. Half measures availed us nothing. We stood at the turning point.

Here are the steps we took, which are suggested as a program of recovery:

1. We admitted we were powerless over alcohol - that our lives had become unmanageable.

2. We came to believe and to accept that we needed strengths and resources beyond our awareness to restore us to sanity.

3. We made a decision to turn our will and our lives over to the collective wisdom of those who have searched before us.

4. We made a searching and fearless inventory of ourselves.

5. We admitted to ourselves, without reservation, and to

154

another human being the exact nature of our wrongs.

6. We were ready to accept help in letting go all defects of character.

7. With humility and openness, we sought to eliminate our shortcomings.

8. We made a list of all persons we had harmed, and became willing to make amends to them all.

9. We made direct amends to such people whenever possible, except when to do so would injure them or others.

10. We continued to take personal inventory and when we were wrong promptly admitted it.

11. We sought through meditation to improve our spiritual awareness and our understanding of the AA way of life and to discover the power to carry out that way of life.

12. Having changed as the result of these steps, we tried to carry this message to alcoholics, and to practice these principles in all our affairs.

Many of us exclaimed, "What an order! I can't go through with it." Do not be discouraged. No one among us has been able to maintain anything like perfect adherence to these principles. We are human and not perfect. The point is, that we are willing to grow along spiritual lines. The principles we have set down are guides to progress. We claim spiritual progress rather than spiritual perfection.

Our description of the alcoholic and personal experiences make clear three pertinent ideas:

(a) That we were alcoholic and could not manage our own lives.

(b) That we needed strength beyond our awareness in order to recover.

(c) That recovery is possible for nearly anyone willing to entrust themselves to this simple way of life.

Adapted from the book *Alcoholics Anonymous®*

Appendix II
Histories of ten agnostic groups in Canada

A Broad Highway

By Gord A
Nelson, British Columbia

Two long time members of AA in the vicinity of Nelson, BC were Shirley R and Gord A, and they had discussed the need for a secular AA group several times since about 2014. Gord had also discussed the possibility with his wife, and they both felt that perhaps Nelson was too small a town for such a meeting, and it could alienate other mainstream members.

Gord was an enthusiastic supporter of AA Agnostica and had visited Toronto, attending several of the agnostic groups there in the spring of 2014. Having attended AA meetings all across the continent, his appraisal of the Toronto agnostic groups was that they were totally AA - warm and welcoming and exactly what was needed for the newly searching problem drinker who had an aversion to the religious flavour of traditional AA. The agnostic meetings felt like old time AA where people connected and attended meetings together, went for coffee after the meeting and went out of their way to drive you home.

In 2015 Cate S and Wayne P started attending the 7 AM Attitude Adjustment group which Gord and Shirley often attended. This tipped the balance. While Shirley already had a home group, she was enthusiastic and helped with the early organization of our agnostic meeting.

We made sure that people understood that we considered this a true AA group by registering with GSO. We had a representative, Wayne, at the October, 2015 District 75 committee meeting for BC / Yukon Area 79. Wayne continues to complete his term as our GSR.

There was some overt criticism of this new meeting, but we didn't let that stop us.

The group conscience has explicitly expressed that ours is an open meeting and that we strongly support AA's singleness of purpose: to attain sobriety and to share the message with those who are likewise afflicted.

The first meeting of A Broad Highway was held on Thursday Nov 5, 2015 at 5:00 PM at the Cellar in Nelson, the meeting venue for almost all of Nelson AA. We have since had attendance of up to 15 people and are a solid group, in for the long haul. We stay active at the District level and our DCM has attended whenever he could.

Our meeting is one hour long.

We open with a moment of silence, remembering those that have helped us and those we may help.

Any announcements? Anyone here for their first or second AA meeting? Anyone coming back?

Any visitors from out of town?

On page 164 of the Big Book, Bill Wilson wrote: "Our book is meant to be suggestive only. We realize we know but a little", and in the Foreword to *Twelve Steps and Twelve Traditions*, he wrote: "AA's Twelve Steps are a group of principles, spiritual in their nature, which, if practiced as a way of life, can expel the obsession to drink and enable the sufferer to become happily and usefully whole." With that in mind, here is a secular version, suggested as a program of recovery. At this point members take turns reading the Bay Area version of the 12 steps as found and adapted from *The Little Book*.

We read the current day's selection from *Beyond Belief* by Joe C of Toronto, and have half a dozen copies on the table for people to follow. We also have copies of *The Little Book*, the AA Big Book, *Twelve Steps and Twelve Traditions* and *Daily Reflections*. After the opening, we use the "popcorn" method of sharing, where we sit in silence until someone wants to share.

We close with the AA Declaration of Responsibility.

Sober Agnostics

By Hilary J
Vancouver, British Columbia

Sober Agnostics, Vancouver, BC, District 26, Area 79, meets every Tuesday at 7 PM in the Activity Room in a church basement at 1440 West 12th Avenue.

The organizing meeting was held in February 2013, hosted by Stephanie S, with Denis K, Michael D and Hilary J attending.

Michael secured us a space at a very reasonable rent. Denis arranged to get the meeting listed in the Vancouver Intergroup directory, and our inaugural meeting was held on Tuesday, May 7, 2013, chaired by Michael. According to Denis K's account in *Don't Tell: Stories and essays by agnostics and atheists in AA*, five men and four women attended the first meeting.

At first, the format was the "uncomfortable silence" model: after the daily reading from Joe C's *Beyond Belief*, the floor was open, and anyone could speak (or not) if and when they felt the urge. Last year, the group decided to change this to "go around in a circle", with the floor re-opened for more informal sharing after everyone has had a chance. We still read from *Beyond Belief*, but have replaced the "Serenity Wish" with the "Responsibility Declaration" to close the meeting. We first used the "agnostic adaptation" of How It Works from the AA Agnostica website, but later revised this to better fit the character of the group.

Our meeting soon attracted the attention of the Vancouver Intergroup operating committee. The Committee chair, Jim J, attended incognito to "see what we were up to", announcing himself at the end of the meeting. When the next edition of the directory was published (September 2013), Sober Agnostics had been deleted.

This precipitated lengthy, sometimes hostile debates at the monthly Intergroup meetings.

Since we had changed the Steps, and did not use the official AA literature, were we really an AA group? Did the operating committee have the authority to decide whether we should be listed? A package was issued to all Intergroup reps to take back to their home groups for group conscience. After months of agonizing debate and delays, the final vote was on whether Intergroup should continue to discuss the matter. The verdict was "No" (January 2014).

However it was eventually decided to have an actual vote on whether or not the Greater Vancouver Intergroup Society would list the agnostic groups. That vote took place on March 21, 2017. In order to have the required two thirds majority, 31 of those present would have to vote in favour.

In the end, 33 voted to "list all groups that wish to be listed". After more than three years of being excluded, we were back in!

Like many groups, our membership has fluctuated greatly over the years. Only a handful of the original members still attend regularly. Most meetings range from 6 to 12 people, and we frequently welcome newcomers, who mainly learn about us from the website. We print business cards and deposit them in strategic locations around the city, and until recently, had a sandwich board sign on the sidewalk outside the meeting (we removed it at the request of the church). These methods have also attracted some newcomers.

Our dear friend, mentor and motivator Denis K passed away in 2016, having enjoyed more than 40 years of sobriety. He was the driving force behind the Vancouver Agnostic AA movement and is still much missed!

We Agnostics

By Andrea M and Sandy T
Nanaimo, British Columbia

We Agnostics Meeting in Nanaimo, BC was formed by two women - one with 27 years and one with 12 years. Our first meeting was on Wednesday, August 13, 2014; Sandy T and Andrea M were the founders, with Michael L joining the group at the first meeting. The location had to be central, had to be accessible, had to NOT be a church and had to be cheap. Luckily there was such a place in Nanaimo, where the non-profit group 7-10 Club has a free breakfast program 6 days a week in a city-owned building. They do not charge the group rent, but gratefully accept the group's donation every month.

The format was borrowed directly from the AA Agnostica website, and we read the extended Preamble explaining the purpose of the meeting. We open with a moment of silence to remember those who are still suffering, and close with the AA Responsibility Declaration. We do not read any AA literature thereby avoiding ALL debates about GOD or gender inclusive language. We have free AA brochures available for newcomers.

From the very beginning the group has been a contributing member to Intergroup's Central Office, District 7, BC/Yukon Area 79 and GSO in New York.

Attendance started small with only 10-15, but after our first year attendance had grown to 30-40 people each week. In May 2016 the group started a Sunday afternoon meeting at 4 PM because the Wednesday night meeting had grown to have 50-60 people. The Sunday afternoon meeting now has a minimum of 15-20 people, and usually everyone gets a chance to share.

We currently have 25 group members and a strong showing at business meetings. All service positions are filled, and the Nanaimo Intergroup - Central Office lists both meetings on their website and printed directories. Our meetings are very well attended, the topics change and the discussion-sharing is rich.

We are very proud to be offering this option in Nanaimo's growing AA community.

Beyond Belief

By Corinne L, Dan L and Neil F
Stony Plain, Alberta

Stony Plain, Alberta's Beyond Belief Group and its 9 AM Saturday Meeting originated in October 2013 when Dan L, Neil F and Corinne L brainstormed at her house about a way to create an inclusive secular AA group that did not try to convert or de-convert anyone and allowed for any individual beliefs or non-beliefs. We also wanted to create a meeting where we were free of religious pressure and AA dogma. To be non-controversial and to avoid the problems Toronto's secular groups encountered in being de-listed by the Toronto Intergroup, we chose to eliminate reading any form of the 12 steps or traditions and to place Conference-approved books on the table we sit around along with a variety of secular recovery books.

Enthusiasm permeated our first small meeting on 16 November 2013 and our meeting attendance over the next five months ranged between two to six people. On 19 April 2014, at the suggestion of Tom G who had just returned from his winter sojourn to the States, we decided to become a registered group. Our New Group Form was completed and submitted to GSO and Area 78 and we were recognized as a registered group in May of 2014. At this point, the group was comprised of five founding members: Corinne L, Dan L, Tom G, Leif P and Neil F. Since then, our membership has fluctuated; at this point we have ten active members and our typical meeting has six to ten attendees.

It is rumored that there are some local AA members who feel that we are not a real AA group because we do not include prayer in our meetings and do not open our meetings by reading from the Big Book or other AAWS Conference-approved literature. Over time, this has prompted AA members to investigate what is going on; at the end of the meeting a number have indicated that they enjoyed our meeting and its format and a couple have said some variation of, "I'm glad I didn't have contempt prior to investigation because you guys have a real meeting ".

We open our meeting with an explanation of our format, which welcomes everyone to an Open Meeting of Alcoholics Anonymous, a safe environment in which there will be no prayer. The AA Preamble, the AA Responsibility Pledge and a reading from the book *Beyond Belief* follow. Discussion is based on the reading or any recovery issue. If there is time left over, we have open discussion until time for announcements and we end with our Serenity Affirmation, "May I have the serenity…"

A number of members of our group felt oppressed by what they felt was overt religiosity and AA dogma expressed in some of the other AA meetings they had attended. We found that after some initial venting, regular participants tend to focus on how to live peaceful sober lives full of sanity and stability. All attendees are safe to express their woes as well as their joys in our meetings without being attacked or told what they should do.

We are extremely fortunate to have several members who have decades of continuous sobriety and service under their belts and are highly respected in our local AA community. They give our group "street cred" as young people might say.

We participate in the District 10 and Area 78 Meetings and contribute financially to both as well as other service entities. In addition, we keep AA brochures stocked at the Serenity Center on behalf of all of the groups that meet there.

To date, the Stony Plain Beyond Belief group consists of a strong core membership with many regular and occasional visitors. A few of our regulars are snowbirds and bugger off for the winter but always return, happy to be back home. If you are in the neighborhood, please join us.

Beyond Belief

By Cathy M, Doreen D, Gayle K
Winnipeg, Manitoba

The first "secular" meeting in Winnipeg, Manitoba, Canada met on January 4, 2016 at the St. Vital United Church, 613 St. Mary's Road. Doreen D and Cathy M had the notion to start this group after attending the 2015 International AA Convention in Atlanta GA.

It was there at a panel entitled "We Agnostics" that they heard speakers discussing aspects of "secular" AA and the need for inclusive, non-denominational meetings of Alcoholics Anonymous. There were many international groups already formed with a focus apart from a "Christian" outlook – new and long term members who recognized storytelling and individual experiences as a power greater than themselves.

After finding the space to meet in the St. Vital church, we (Gayle K, Doreen D and Cathy M) commenced regular, closed AA meetings, using a format that welcomed freethinkers and other seekers, and those who worked with other agnostics, atheists or non-believers in recovery. Taking a page from others before us, we were mindful of remaining in the AA fold and stressing the importance of the steps (however one interprets the steps), sponsorship and service.

After six months, Beyond Belief registered with New York AA office (June 2016) and was listed on the Winnipeg AA meeting list in September. Given the small number of regular attendees (5 - 8) at our group, we rotate the responsibility of opening the meeting space and chairing meetings – splitting duties and positions as necessary to promote our group with Intergroup and General Service (Area 80, District 7). We have had two business meetings to date to structure our group and to focus on growing our membership.

Two of our members attended the WAAFT Convention in Austin, Texas in November 2016 to meet and share with others in this international AA community. The message is that AA is slow to welcome changes or alternatives to the original 12 Steps and our acceptance will take time and patience.

At this writing we are pleased at our one year anniversary and continue to seed greater exposure through word of mouth.

All are Welcome Group

By Steve V, Dave J and Bill K
Windsor, Ontario

The All Are Welcome group of Alcoholics Anonymous in Windsor, Ontario started with a chance meeting between two of the founding members at the We Agnostics meeting on a November 2015 Tuesday evening in Toronto. Dave J, from Windsor was in Toronto on business and to attend the meeting and met Steve V who mentioned in his sharing he was moving to Windsor in March 2016. The two chatted after the meeting and agreed to meet up and talk about starting an agnostic / atheist / freethinkers meeting once Steve moved to Windsor. After Steve moved to Windsor, he met with Dave, Bill K and John T and discussed setting up a meeting together. They agreed on a format that was modeled after the We Agnostics meeting and held the first All Are Welcome Group meeting on Saturday May 14, 2016 with 14 people in attendance.

One of the interesting things about the formation of the group was approaching the priest of the Catholic Church that would end up being the venue where the group meets. When told of the idea of starting the first AA agnostic / atheist / freethinkers meeting in the Windsor area, the priest was very supportive. In fact, he identified as a "friend of Bill W" and attends the meeting once or twice a month himself!

Each Saturday it's a topic discussion selected by those in attendance. Topics range from Step 1 to "Loneliness", "Gratitude" or "Handling relationships while being sober". Frequently our attendance is six to ten people and sometimes fewer. The size of the group makes for some intimate sharing and sometimes people simply share about what they're currently dealing with rather than any of the three topics.

The make-up of those attending our group is diverse. We have agnostics, atheists and believers who are attending in order to escape some of the dogma and rigid thinking they sometimes find at some other AA meetings. We have lots of people who have been visiting the Windsor area and came to check out our meeting not realizing we're an agnostic meeting. They tend to be pleasantly surprised to find we're really not much different from "regular" AA meetings and end up enjoying themselves. We also have some people who like our meeting but come perhaps once every one or two months.

Six months since starting our meeting we as a group have decided to raise more awareness about our group in the Windsor Area so we're planning to attend our first District meeting this month to let other AA members know about us. We have some pamphlets printed up to give out to various DSR's so they can take them back to their groups. As well, we're starting to go to other AA meetings here in the area to make an announcement about our group and to also leave pamphlets. We're really not sure how we will be received but we're willing to take this risk under the belief there must be other AA members like us who want to get and stay sober while still being able to keep their own beliefs and not having to accept anyone else's beliefs.

We love our All Are Welcome Group and are confident and encouraged as we move forward.

The Broader Path AA Group

By Don M and Dennis K
Odessa, Ontario

During a conversation in 2015, Martin D and I (Don M), confided that we were atheists and felt increasingly uncomfortable in some AA meetings. With a third member of the fellowship, an agnostic named Dennis K, we formed a Steering Committee to start an agnostic / atheist AA meeting in the Kingston area. Resources found online at AA Agnostica proved quite helpful.

Participants at the meeting would study both Conference-approved and non-AA materials related to recovery from alcoholism. All comers in search of sobriety were welcome. Twelve people attended our first gathering on 8 July 2015 at the Emmanuel United Church in Odessa, Ontario. John B, a believer with 20 years in AA, came to pray for us, eventually joined, and embarked on a spiritual journey that has forged his belief in a power greater than himself that he calls LOVE.

Over the next six months our Group Conscience agreed on a secular set of 12 Steps for internal use. By then we had 13 members representing more than 200 years of sobriety. Some were new, while one had been sober over 45 years.

In December of 2015, our Group presented its first medallion to Fred B for five years of continuous sobriety. Fred didn't expect many people at his celebration but was delighted that there was standing room only that night.

The Group contacted the Kingston Public Information Committee to request a Website listing. We were welcomed by Connie K, Bill H, the webmaster, and Jeff L, Chair. They were pleased to have a secular alternative to offer suffering alcoholics who contacted the website but indicated an aversion to regular AA meetings because of the "God thing". To ensure that the hand of AA would always be there, they immediately listed The Broader Path.

However, when news of our secular Group reached the District 36 Table there was some apprehension. In August 2015 we had registered with GSO and, in October 2015, received service number 716632. Despite this, a motion was made to remove The Broader Path from the website and deny our GSR a seat at the Table. District 36 facilitated an e-mail debate. Some letters of support advocated inclusion while others passionately promoted exclusion. We experienced the timeless wisdom of placing principles before personalities.

In December 2015, the motion to de-list our Group fell just short of a 2/3 majority. A subsequent motion placed a moratorium on further efforts to de-list The Broader Path until January 2017. We are hopeful that ongoing experience with our group, and the results of the Ontario Human Rights Tribunal, will resolve this divisive controversy.

As we enter 2017, The Broader Path continues to grow, and to attract newcomers. We neither endorse nor oppose atheism or any religion. Our secular Group carries the message that suffering alcoholics can find sobriety in Alcoholics Anonymous without having to accept anyone else's beliefs or deny their own. Love and tolerance of others is our code.

The Secular Step Meeting

By Jo-Anne K
Toronto, Ontario

The Secular Step Meeting (now Beyond Belief Secular Step Meeting) was started out of concern that the newcomer to atheist, agnostic, and free thinker groups were not being introduced to the steps of the AA program. Not every person that comes to AA needs to embrace the 12 steps but it was felt that at least they should have an introduction to them. Each person can then decide for themselves whether the 12 steps will be a part of their recovery. Many people in secular groups, as well as mainstream AA groups, stay sober by working the 12 Steps and many stay sober without working the Steps.

I mentioned this to other members of the group and a small working group was formed. This group included Genevieve F, Amelia C, Steph G, Brian N, and myself, Jo-Anne K. We wanted this to be an organic process which defined the needs of members. Brian created a survey to discern who was interested in having a step discussion and on what day and what time. Compiling the surveys, we found that Monday at 7:00 PM seemed to be the best day and time to have this step discussion. And so, on Jan 4 the first meeting of Secular Step Meeting was held at Ontario Institute for Studies in Education (OISE).

The group was (and still is) a work in progress and we needed to be flexible and make changes based on the needs of the members.

The working group had decided to use the 12 Steps as they had been originally written, God and all. At that very first meeting this was discovered to be problematic. A number of people were very upset that they had come to a secular meeting and were still being confronted with literature that contained the word god. One person was actually in tears. The working group decided to use an alternative version of the 12 steps and developed a version of the 12 steps to be used at this group.

The original format of the meeting was to have a 10 minute speaker on one of the steps each week and that would be followed with a group discussion. However we quickly ran out of people in agnostic, atheists and freethinker groups that had experience with the steps and were available to speak.

It was decided that we would read from one of the many texts written on the 12 steps and follow this with discussion. This is the current format but we have widened the literature selection, changing books with each go-round of the steps. There are many texts written explaining the 12 steps, from many different perspectives. We hope to get it across to members that they can interpret the steps and all of the other AA literature in a way that helps them to stay sober.

The wording of the steps is not as important as the principles which inspire them; it is these principles that guide us in our continued sobriety. In April 2016 it was decided that the Secular Step meeting would become a part of the Beyond Belief Group. This made sense for financial and logistical reasons. Room bookings at the university could be made for all three of the Beyond Belief meetings at the same time, literature could be ordered in bulk etc.

This meeting has not always been well attended. However, now that the Beyond Belief Group has been re-listed in the GTA meeting list of Alcoholics Anonymous that has changed. The first Monday after the Beyond Belief meetings could be found in the online Greater Toronto Area general AA list, five newcomers showed up at the step meeting. Three of these were people who had previously been to mainstream AA and two of them were at their very first meeting.

It is our hope that this Secular Step Meeting of the Beyond Belief group will continue to grow and provide an option for those members wishing to discuss the 12 Steps.

Freethinkers Group

By Tom C and Cecelia R
Ajax, Ontario

In August of 2015 Tom C and Cecelia R were in attendance at the Monday Night Whitby Freethinkers Meeting and started discussing the possibility of having another Freethinkers meeting in the district and that Ajax might be a possible location. Whitby Freethinkers was only on Monday nights and another meeting throughout the week would have benefit.

A discussion was held with the co-founders of Whitby Freethinkers Craig C and Bob K for their thoughts and if we could follow their format. It was given full support by them and the search was on to find a place in Ajax to hold the meeting.

Seeing that the Library seemed the most appropriate place to start, that's what we did. Ajax Library was contacted and a room made available at minimal cost. The library was thought to be a great resource available for folks after the meeting to do some research on what was discussed that evening.

Tom and Cecelia discussed requirements... coffee, cookies, and it was agreed that most folk do bring their own coffee and at this time this expense could be eliminated until the group got going financially. The first meeting would be held on a Thursday night at 7 PM (later changed to 7:30 PM), on October 8, 2016.

The format was the selection of two topics and a step discussion. With support from some of the members of the Whitby Freethinkers group our first meeting got underway. Cecelia brought some of her home baked goods that were totally appreciated... We had some folks from Toronto and the surrounding areas. A small group of the members started to go for coffee afterwards at Deb's Cafe across the street from the library and the fellowship flourished in the after meeting coffee gatherings.

A small core has stayed together with Ajax Freethinkers and the discussions are open and honest and very considerate. We are part of the Lakeshore Districts (26-28) and Eastern Ontario Area 83. We have yet to inform our local Intergroup of our group meeting as some members wish to fully discuss it more. However, word of mouth is out there and we get different people showing up because we are listed on the AA Agnostica website.

The group is welcoming and willing to help others. The meeting is very thoughtful and considerate to all those who attend, including those who believe in a God or a higher power. We endeavour to be sensitive to the needs of all.

The Only Requirement Group

By Reed H
Halifax, Nova Scotia

In the spring of 2011, a loyal AA member in Halifax, Nova Scotia had a moment of clarity: As far as he was concerned, there was no such thing as a supernatural higher power called God.

For the next few months, this member continued to go to AA meetings but struggled. It had suddenly become a lot harder to find comfort and meaning in AA with its strong religious influences and pressures to believe.

The member figured there must be others in the local AA community who were non-believers, and perhaps some of them were also struggling to reconcile their beliefs within the program. With the approval of the editor, a one-line note and contact email address was placed in the area AA newsletter.

Within a few days of publication, the member had been contacted by three other members. The four of them agreed to meet for coffee, and the idea for a non-religious AA meeting hatched.

Within a few weeks, the group had a meeting time and location, as well as a name: The Only Requirement Group. The group made a conscious decision not to be only for atheists and agnostics. Instead, it was open to everyone of all beliefs, however, the only thing not welcome was religion.

The group also decided to adopt interpretations of AA's 12 Steps and 12 Traditions which did not include references to God. Adoption of these altered Steps and Traditions turned out to be a pivotal decision which divided the local AA community.

Once established, The Only Requirement Group approached the Central Service Committee and requested inclusion in the area AA newsletter and meeting list. When the meeting's adapted 12 Steps and Traditions were presented, numerous representatives of area meetings balked and concluded that we were not a real AA meeting and that we should not be recognized as such.

It was decided that the issue of inclusion should be brought back the group level for consideration before the Central Service committee held a vote on the matter. In subsequent Central Service meetings, passionate arguments against inclusion of the group were heard. The committee overwhelmingly voted against inclusion.

Nevertheless, there were a few members of the Central Service committee who, despite their own beliefs, recognized the importance of a non-religious meeting lest AA turn away still suffering alcoholics.

Although disappointed with the decision, the group maintained its regularly scheduled meetings, and membership grew despite the lack of acknowledgement in local AA publications.

About a year after the group was voted down by Central Service, inclusion was once again brought to the committee for consideration. By this time, the Group's supporters on the committee had grown considerably, and even though it was voted down a second time, it lost by only one vote.

Group members were once again disappointed by the result but encouraged by the closeness of the vote. For the next year, the group continued to plug along and pick up new members.

The group also made efforts to participate in service work such as answering the weekend AA phone, host meetings at the local detox facility, and make financial contributions to various service levels of AA.

About a year after the second vote, the Group was invited to participate in a third vote by Central Service Committee. This time, the votes tipped strongly in favour of bringing The Only Requirement Group into the fold.

It was a very welcome result for group members, who were especially thankful to a small group of Central Service Committee members that fought long and hard for the group despite their own personal convictions and strong opposition from fellow committee members.

That was a little over a year ago and The Only Requirement Group continues to thrive as acknowledged members of the local AA community. The Group, now in its sixth year, meets on Sunday nights at 7:30 PM at Club 24, 3 Dundas Street in Downtown Dartmouth, across the bridge from Halifax.

The group is proud to provide an alternative to traditional AA, while at the same time embracing the principles of a program that helps save friends and family from the ravages of alcoholism.

All are welcome!

Appendix III
Five Stories from AA Agnostica

The "Don't Tell" Policy in AA

By Roger C

There often seems to be an unofficial policy in Alcoholics Anonymous especially for nonbelievers at AA meetings: "Don't Tell."

It is a policy imposed by just a few but rarely challenged.

If you are an atheist, agnostic, humanist or secularist you had best keep your lack of belief in a deity to yourself. (And yet, according to Bill W., AA is officially for everyone "regardless of their belief or lack of belief").

Here's an example of the problem: John M tells about how easily everyone accepts it when an AA speaker says, "I owe this to my Higher Power whom I choose to call God."

"No problem here!" John writes, and he continues:

> However, a long standing sober member of my home group once told me that when she was sharing at a closed meeting she spoke of her higher power "whom I choose not to call God." The looks she got, the raised eyebrows, the shuffling of fannies in the chairs indicated to her that her declaration was a problem for many in the room. At that moment, it felt to her as if she had uttered a blasphemy.

"Don't Tell." That's the policy for nonbelievers in AA.

There are three main ways to be "outed" as an agnostic in Alcoholics Anonymous:

> 1. By sharing, as John's friend did.

> 2. By removing the word "God" from the 12 Step program of recovery. In 1939 the words "as we understood Him" were added to "God" in the suggested 12 Steps. Today, for many nonbelievers, that compromise is not enough. The word "God" is removed while the intent of the Step is maintained.

> 3. By declining to recite the Lord's Prayer at the end of an AA meeting.

Some readers will be familiar with the "Don't Ask Don't Tell" policy which was for some time the official United States policy on homosexuals serving in the military. The policy prohibited discriminating against or harassing closeted homosexual or bisexual service members, while barring openly gay or lesbian persons from military service.

The "Don't Tell" part of the policy meant that if you didn't let on that you were a gay or a lesbian then you could still be a member in good standing of the armed forces. If you admitted you were a homosexual, however, then you were kicked out.

The "Don't Ask" part meant that nobody could ask you if you were a gay or a lesbian. Or even a bi-sexual. And the top brass couldn't investigate to find out; they couldn't go to your home, ask your friends or follow you to bars or meetings.

There doesn't appear to be a "Don't Ask" part in this policy in AA.

A rumour circulated in the Toronto area that there was a new AA group in Richmond Hill which, although it read the traditional 12 Steps of AA, also shared an interpretation of some of the steps without the "God" word.

Four self-appointed AA police officers decided to investigate and showed up at a Widening Our Gateway meeting on Sunday, November 20, 2011, and sure enough, they concluded, there was evidence of tampered Steps.

A month later, on December 20, one of these detectives presented a motion at Intergroup that Widening Our Gateway be suspended from Intergroup membership for changing the Steps.

The motion will be voted on at the next Intergroup meeting.

Meanwhile back in the United States military, the "Don't Ask Don't Tell" policy finally came to an end on September 20, 2011. It took a while for the new rules to take effect but on December 21, in an article headlined "Gay Navy Couple Torpedo Don't Ask Don't Tell with First Kiss," the San Diego News reported on an historic moment. Petty Officer Marissa Gaeta and her partner Citalic Snell became the first gay couple in Navy history to share the "first kiss" moment when the navy ship USS Oak Hill returned from Central America.

The News further reported that Gaeta told a gaggle of reporters: "It's something new, that's for sure. It's nice to be able to be myself. It's been a long time coming."

Will the "Don't Tell" policy at AA meetings ever come to an end?

Of course.

AA as a fellowship will meet this new challenge or, as Joe, a founding member of an agnostic AA group put it: "My bold prediction is that if AA doesn't accommodate change and diversify, our 100th anniversary will be a fellowship of men and women with the same stature and relevance as the Mennonites; charming, harmless and irrelevant."

Remember, everything is always impossible until, well, it turns out to be both possible and normal.

It's been a long time coming but nonbelievers will yet have a place in the rooms of AA.

In the meantime, for God's sake:

"Don't Tell."

Responsibility is Our Theme

By Roger C

Bill W spoke at the General Service Conference held in New York City in April, 1965. The Conference theme was "Responsibility to Those We Serve".

AA was thirty years old. Bill was 70 years old. It was a period of reflection for him. "We old-timers are a vanishing breed," he said of the early members of AA. "The greater part of us have gone out into the sunset of this world."

He expressed the hope that the disappearing early AAers had left the members of the day a heritage sufficient to their needs, one which could be "enlarged and enriched".

Bill was preparing for the 30th Anniversary International Convention to be held later that year in July in Toronto. Much of the spirit of the Conference would also prevail at the Convention, where the theme would be, simply, "Responsibility", and Bill would repeat much of this speech.

Bill looked back over the years; he did a bit of an inventory of AA's history, "the better to reveal the areas in which we can improve ourselves".

"Without much doubt, a million alcoholics have approached AA during the last thirty years", he said. Estimating that "350,000 of us are now recovered from our malady" through the fellowship of AA, he continued, "So we can very soberly ask ourselves what became of the 600,000 who did not stay".

No doubt some alcoholics "cannot be reached because they are not hurt enough, others because they are hurt too much. Many sufferers have mental and emotional complications that seem to foreclose their chances", Bill acknowledged.

But what about all the others?

"How much and how often did we fail them?" he asked.

"Our very first concern should be with those sufferers that we are still unable to reach."

He had some sense of the failings of the fellowship he had helped launch and which he still clearly revered. One of the themes for his talk was one he had broached before: a growing rigidity in AA.

He referred directly to a contingent within the fellowship which, often unwittingly, made it difficult for an increasingly large number of people to feel comfortable in the rooms of AA. "It is a historical fact", he said, "that practically all groupings of men and women tend to become dogmatic. Their beliefs and practices harden and sometimes freeze. This is a natural and almost inevitable process."

He discussed some of the ways that this rigidity could harm the fellowship.

"In no circumstances should we feel that Alcoholics Anonymous is the know-all and do-all of alcoholism", Bill said, referring to the work of other organizations in the United States and Canada engaged in research, alcohol education and rehabilitation.

"Research has already come up with significant and helpful findings. And research will do far more."

"Those engaged in education are carrying the message that alcoholism is an illness, that something can be done about it."

Bill then talked about the growth of rehabilitation facilities in North America and the number of alcoholics treated by these agencies. "True, their approach is often different from our own", he said.

"But what does that matter", he asked, "when the greater part of them are or could be entirely willing to cooperate with AA?"

"Too often, I believe, we have deprecated and even derided these projects of our friends."

"So we should very seriously ask ourselves how many alcoholics have gone on drinking simply because we have failed to cooperate in good spirit with all these other agencies whether they be good, bad or indifferent. Assuredly no alcoholic should go mad or die simply because he did not come straight to AA in the first place."

Bill was of the view that hardened or frozen beliefs and practices were dangerous in AA. "Simply because we have convictions that work very well for us, it becomes quite easy to assume that we have all of the truth."

"Whenever this brand of arrogance develops", he warned, "we are sure to become aggressive. We demand agreement with us. We play God."

"This isn't good dogma. This is very bad dogma. It could be especially destructive for us of AA to indulge in this sort of thing."

Bill defended the right of all AAers to have their own beliefs and to be able to freely express them.

"All people must necessarily rally to the call of their own particular convictions and we of AA are no exception." Moreover, he continued, "all people should have the right to voice their convictions".

Bill then returned to the subject of those who had come into AA but not stayed. "Newcomers are approaching us at the rate of tens of thousands yearly. They represent almost every belief and attitude imaginable."

"We have atheists and agnostics", he said. "We have people of nearly every race, culture and religion."

And then Bill got to the heart of his message of responsibility.

> In AA we are supposed to be bound together in the kinship of a universal suffering. Therefore the full liberty to practice any creed or principle or therapy should be a first consideration. Hence let us not pressure anyone with individual or even collective views. Let us instead accord to each other the respect that is due to every human being as he tries to make his way towards the light. Let us always try to be inclusive rather than exclusive. Let us remember that each alcoholic among us is a member of AA, so long as he or she so declares.

Towards the end of his address, Bill commented on how difficult it has been for AA to grow at important moments in its history. "Our fears and reluctances and rebellions have been extreme each time we have been faced with great turning points in this society", he said.

"Let us never fear needed change", he concluded. "Once a need becomes clearly apparent in an individual, a Group, or in AA as a whole, it has long since been found out that we cannot afford to sit still and look the other way."

Hallowed be the Big Book?

By Laurie A.

The Preface to the fourth edition of the Big Book notes, "Because this book has become the basic text for our Society and has helped such large numbers of alcoholic men and women to recovery, there exists strong sentiment against any radical changes being made in it. Therefore, the first portion of this volume, describing the AA recovery program, has been left untouched ..."

That's the problem.

Despite the book's own caveats, e.g., "Our book is meant to be suggestive only. We realise we know only a little. God (*sic*) will constantly reveal more to you and to us ...", and the dust jacket description of the book as the (neutral), "basic text of Alcoholics Anonymous", fundamentalist members treat it as the literal, revealed, inviolable word of God; commandments, not suggestions. As Joe C. observed of The Doctor's Opinion in his book of daily reflections *Beyond Belief* (November 24), "Critics inside AA would have preferred that the 1976 and 2004 reprint offered AA members a second opinion (because) *more has been revealed...* It is not disrespectful to those who have come before us and done so much for us to show that the courage they taught us has enabled us to reach further."

No doubt AA co-founder Bill W., who supervised the compilation of the first edition of the Big Book when he was less than four years sober, would tell the story differently were he writing today. He recognised that:

> *As time passes our book literature has the tendency to get more and more frozen, a tendency for conversion into something like dogma, a human trait I am afraid we can do little about. We may as well face the fact that AA will always have its fundamentalists, its absolutists, and its relativists. (Letter quoted by Ernest Kurtz in* Not-God: A History of Alcoholics Anonymous*)*

Each faction will find justification in its pages. As Joe C. points out, "Our biases predispose us to seek evidence that supports our (opening) positions and deny even overwhelming evidence to the contrary. Open minds, sceptical of even our most heartfelt convictions, are our best defense against our own tendency towards confirmation bias." (*Beyond Belief*, December 7)

For example, textual zealots tell us that there are many "musts" in the Big Book, from 55 references to 103 depending on the "authority" counting them! They neglect to add that in all cases but one the "must" in the first 164 pages is preceded by the word "we", so for the must to apply to me I would have to be part of the "we". The people who wrote the book were recording what they had to do to get sober ("We merely have an approach that works for us"); they were not telling anyone else what to do. On page 20 the book says, "If you are an alcoholic who wants to get over it, you may already be asking – 'What do I have to do?' It is the purpose of this book to answer such questions specifically. *We shall tell you what we have done*" (emphasis added). The logical, grammatical answer to, "What do I have to do?" is, "You have to do this", but our pioneers gave us a text that is descriptive, not prescriptive. In Alcoholics *Anonymous Comes of Age* (AACoA), Bill W. records that when 400 copies of the first draft of the Big Book were circulated for comments to anyone they knew who was concerned about the problem of alcoholism, the psychiatrist Dr. Howard made a "critically important" suggestion:

> *He pointed out that the text was too full of the words "you" and "must" and suggested that we substitute wherever possible such expressions as "we ought" or "we should". His idea was to remove all forms of coercion, to put our fellowship on a "we ought" basis instead of a "you must" basis... Dr Silkworth and Dr. Tiebout gave us similar advice.*

So the redactors were at work from the very beginning and in the light of continuing revelation there is no reason for us in 2015 not to apply the scalpels of hermeneutics and form criticism to AA's "scriptures" too – indeed, it is our responsibility and duty to do so.

Far from being a text book of incontrovertible instructions or rules the Big Book is, in fact, a story book, it says so in its very title, *Alcoholics Anonymous – The story of how many thousands of men and women have recovered from alcoholism*. The dust cover of the fourth edition quotes a letter written by Bill W. in 1953:

> *The story section of the Big Book is far more important than most of us think. It is our principal means of identifying with the reader outside AA; it is the written*

*equivalent of hearing speakers at an AA meeting; it is
our show window of results.*

In AACoA he wrote, "The story section could identify us with the distant reader in a way that the text itself (first 164 pages) might not." Kurtz noted, "From its beginnings and still today, the philosophy and spirituality – the healing – of AA is transmitted primarily by the practice of story-telling, of telling a particular kind of story the very format of which inculcates a way of thinking that shapes a particular way of life." (NCCA Blue Book, 1986).

So, here's a classic story about addiction. The wind challenged the sun to a duel. "I'm stronger than you. See that man on the common? I bet you I can rip the cloak from his back." The sun replied, "Do your worst." So the wind summoned all its strength and blew clouds across the sun, the sky darkened, it became menacingly cold. The man wrapped the cloak round himself. The wind blew a mighty gale and tried to tear the man's cloak from him. In panic, the man clung on and wrapped the cloak ever tighter. Exhausted, the wind gave up. Now the sun came out from behind the clouds and said, "Let me try." Its rays felt pleasant on the man's face. He relaxed and as the sun warmed him he loosened his cloak, took it off and slung it over his arm.

As in Aesop's fable, the tension in AA between those who cling to the delusional security of the straitjacket and those who wear their sobriety like a loose cloak has been there from the start. In AACoA Bill W. describes how the conservatives (who thought the Big Book should be Christian in doctrinal sense), liberals and radicals wrestled to have their interpretation of the program take precedence. "The liberals (the largest contingent) were dead set against any other theological proposition (than the word God); they would have nothing to do with doctrinal issues (because the straight religious approach had worked in relatively few cases)." Then Bill adds, "But the atheists and agnostics, our radical left wing were... to make a tremendously important contribution." They wanted "a psychological book which would lure the alcoholic in. Once in, the prospect could take God or leave Him alone as he wished." And by inserting the phrase *as we understood Him* after the word God in the Steps "our atheists and agnostics... widened the gateway so that all who suffer might pass through, regardless of their belief or *lack of belief*." (original emphasis).

Such all-inclusive practice is lost in current narrow legal rulings which seek to define AA as a quasi-religion. Never mind Bill's protestations that, "As a society we must never become so vain as to suppose that

186

we are authors and inventors of a new religion", and "The atheist may stand up in an AA meeting still denying the Deity... in such an atmosphere the orthodox, and the unbeliever mix happily together..." (extracts from *As Bill Sees It*, 158 and 253). A posting on the AA History Lovers website (12/9/14) noted:

> *High level courts use a three part test to determine if the wall of separation (between Church and State) has been violated... They took a long look at the Big Book and its 200 references to God; a look at the 12 Steps and their unmistakeable references to God; the prayers at AA meetings; and based on a full examination of these, ruled that AA doctrines and practices must be viewed as religious. Because multiple high level courts have ruled uniformly on this matter these rulings now constitute "clearly established" law in the US.*

That's the trouble with treating our texts as set in stone dogma; for as we know, "The only requirement for AA membership is a desire to stop drinking." There is no requirement on anyone to read, let alone study, the Big Book or the 12 &12, to practice the Steps, to believe in God, or to pray. Treatment centers which *do* require clients to take the Steps as part of their admission contract mire AA in controversy.

In the 1980s AA in Great Britain was left a substantial legacy in a will. To comply with AA's seventh tradition the GB general service board trustees declined the legacy. The lawyer concerned "challenged our right, as a charity to refuse monies and gave notice to pursue the matter through the courts. Losing our charitable status could lead to the forfeiture of all the Fellowship's assets... the only solution was to submit a Bill to Parliament which would change the law and allow us to decline legacies gifts etc." (Letter from Jim H., GSB chairman, in "Share", the GB Fellowship's national magazine, March 1986)

In drafting the legislation, which was enacted in law as the Alcoholics Anonymous (Dispositions) Act 1986, the civil servants wrote their own preamble describing AA as "an inchoate fellowship whose members seek to overcome their addiction to alcohol by the practice and adherence to a code of principles which have evolved empirically since the fellowship was founded." Inchoate means: just beginning, not fully formed or developed. We're a work in progress. And as David Sack, MD, said in "Psychology Today", "AA will doubtless continue to evolve". "Spearheads of God's ever-advancing creation", as the Big Book says. William White and Ernest Kurtz saw "diversification within

AA as an inevitable process of adaptation to the increasingly diverse religious and cultural contexts inherent in the fellowship's worldwide growth." And in *Not-God* Ernie opined, "AA shall survive so long as its message remains that of the not-God-ness of the wholeness of accepted limitation; and this itself shall endure so long as AA's spiritualisers and its liberals – its 'right' and its 'left' – maintain in mutual respect the creative tension that arises from their willingness to participate even with others of so different assumptions in the shared *honesty of mutual vulnerability openly acknowledged* (original emphasis)".

We need no iron-clad dogma to bind us together. As Bill W. said "In AA we have only two disciplinarians – great suffering and great love; we need no others."

The wind and the sun.

Father of We Agnostics Dies

By Shawn M

I learned tonight that my AA sponsor, Charlie P, passed away in Austin, Texas at the age of 98.

Within recovery communities, one hears much about sponsors. Charlie was both a son of a gun and a saint. Also, the most spiritual man I have ever encountered. That is really saying something about a guy who claimed to be a raging atheist (more on that later).

Many years ago I was "meeting shopping" and in the Los Angeles AA Directory I noticed a meeting called "We Agnostics." There is a chapter in the AA Big Book titled "We Agnostics." In essence, the chapter emphasizes that all drunks come into AA as agnostics and godless but, over time, they rid themselves of that ridiculous concept and see the path towards a Higher Power (code speak for the more commonly used word – God). I thought this "We Agnostics" meeting was either one of two things, a Big Book thumpers meeting or – just maybe - something more interesting. It was indeed more interesting and was located on Barrington Avenue in a big old wood home which was part of the Unitarian Fellowship.

My first meeting there truly made me see the unique, complex components that make up the AA fellowship. This was a group of people that did not subscribe to any notion of canned theology or cultish adherence to anything besides this: "no matter what" one does not put alcohol anywhere near the lips or nostrils. Also, if craving or life itself made you feel like jumping out of your skin, you must pick up the phone and talk with another meeting member. We help each other "no matter what." That was the guiding principle of the LA We Agnostics AA group. Simple concept.

At the end of this meeting an old guy, obviously from NYC, asked me if I was a real alcoholic. I answered in the affirmative. He handed me a piece of paper that looked like one of the slips from a fortune cookie. This guy, Charlie, told me to call him sometime and we'd chat about the Higher Power stuff or anything else about being an alcoholic in the rooms of AA. By the way, the piece of fortune cookie paper he handed me simply said "Charlie" and had a seven digit phone number (he assumed, even then, everyone still lived in the 213 area code). Charlie had brought the AA We Agnostics format to California.

I still have that little slip of paper.

I called Charlie. It was a journey speaking with Charlie. After a month I asked Charlie to sponsor me and he laid out his ground rules. The criteria were, for me, stern and disciplined. This man was not into holding my hand.

He was not an easy sponsor. Doing the Steps with Charlie was hardly a warm, pleasant experience. Brutal in fact. Much better than almost any shrink I had ever encountered and overwhelmingly wise. That was my first Steps go around. Subsequent redoing of the Steps work proved simply enlightening with Charlie. It helped keep me sober then and still does now.

As the years passed, I watched Charlie perform countless acts of real kindness - without an audience. For example: I was at meeting when a deeply disturbed schizophrenic whose personal hygiene was lacking raised his hand and asked for a meal and a ride to a shelter. Charlie quietly took the man and led him out the door – and then into his car. Nobody noticed but me. Not a word was spoken about it. The personal hygiene deficient man kept coming around and the same routine continued for well over a year. Once he (the lacking-hygiene man) showed up clean shaven with clean clothes and looking nourished and healthy. Charlie's doing. This is but one small example. Charlie gave again and again – without looking for attention. To him, having acts of kindness witnessed or acknowledged somehow cheapened the act.

He was not merely about the 12th Step but adhering to a life of giving of oneself – always with unconditional love.

Charlie claimed to be a staunch atheist. His heritage was Jewish but unlike many atheistic Jews, Charlie did not observe the holidays or traditions. That would have been a treasonous act to Charlie. Yet, in later years, after endless hours discussing the definitions of God from the perspective of many belief systems and the nature of the universe from a philosophical stance, Charlie said to me that he had discovered a definition of "God" that he could tolerate. That power greater than himself was the "E" in the equation "$E=mc^2$."

That worked for Charlie and I can embrace his logic.

Charlie's higher purpose and power was the act of loving and all the Energy (the "E" in "$E=mc^2$" equation) contained throughout the universe (both known and unknown). Charlie gave unselfishly and saved countless lives. He did not care to keep score. He was a very devoted loving husband, father, grandfather and great-great-grandfather. Charlie was significant contributor. He saved lives and reinstalled the ability to experience joy into many hearts. He was a holy man.

Charlie had a good run. A life worth living and I am forever grateful to have known this man.

In honor of Charlie, let's never forget the "no matter what" principle of the Los Angeles We Agnostics. My salute and love to Charlie P.

———

Charlie Polacheck, AA founder of "We Agnostics" in Los Angeles, California in 1978 and in Austin, Texas in 2001, passed away on February 27, 2012, after a year of failing health. He was 98 years old and had 41 years of sobriety in AA.

He had many sponsees and affected the lives of many people in AA. In response to Shawn's post, others have shared their knowledge of Charlie:

An elder statesman (by Richard N): As an "elder statesman" of the fellowship, he was never demanding, always accepting. He got all teary-eyed when I told him about my estranged daughter's phone call, after several years of not speaking to me, and then more years of my successful sobriety. She said, "I feel like I've got my Daddy back." As a loving father himself, he really identified with that. Charlie was a Jew and definitely an atheist, so I don't think the Vatican will canonize him any time soon. But in my loving memory he will always be Saint Charlie.

Candles and Charlie (by Sandra B.): I remember Charlie from my early days in sobriety and I knew he was an atheist. Started We Agnostics group and was one of the best AA members to ever have graced the earth. I call myself a Christian and I can't hold a candle to Charlie. RIP Charlie P.

He made a difference (by Bruce K.): My life is infinitely richer having known and loved Charlie P. He made a huge difference in my life, and the lives of countless others. He taught us the true meaning of living rigorously honest, consistently responsible, and unconditionally loving lives. And this very public atheist was truly one of the happiest and most spiritual people I've ever known. Those of us fortunate enough to have known him will carry little bits of Charlie's message and love with us, and we'll pass it on to others so that they also can also benefit from Charlie's experience, strength and hope. Thank you Charlie P.

191

He was legit (by kkash): Charlie. My friend. He lived the richest life of anyone I have ever known. He was brilliant, always cheerful, adored by his family, admired by his friends. Charlie shared his secret to living well often and it was this: "To live well, practice these principles – rigorous honesty, unconditional love, and consistent responsibility." He was legit.

His legacy continues to help (Nick H.): I met Charlie when he moved to Austin in 2000. He also handed me one of his pieces of paper with his name and phone number. During his last 12 years in Austin he became an icon (as it were) of the AA community in Austin and was loved by many all along the belief continuum. Through his influence the number of freethinkers meetings in Austin went from 0 to 6 per week. He has directly and indirectly helped and his legacy continues to help many people who would normally have walked away from a less tolerant AA.

Charlie remained active in the program, holding AA meetings at his bedside and receiving AA visitors up to the last week of his life. Two memorial services were held for him, one at the Northland AA Club in Austin, Texas and a second in Los Angeles, California.

We Are Not Saints

By Roger C

My name is Roger and I am an alcoholic.

It was snowing on Friday evening, the last day of November, in downtown Toronto. I didn't know that until I hauled my bicycle out of the porch and onto the driveway.

It made me a bit nervous. I would have to ride almost three kilometres (two miles, for those south of the border). It didn't matter though; it was an important meeting and I very much wanted to be a part of it.

It was after 7 PM and dark. I attached lights to the front and back of the bike, a flashing red one on the rear fender. Snowflakes slapped against my face as I began to peddle my way. There weren't many people on the streets as I wheeled the bike past Danforth Avenue, through Monarch Park, and under the railroad tracks onto Gerrard Street. When I got to the Unitarian Universalist Congregation on Hiawatha Road I could see Chuck waiting at the door.

"Hi Chuck," I said.

"Hi Roger. The door locks automatically so we need someone to keep it open for others."

"I'll be the greeter then," I said. "Am I the first?"

"Yep," he said.

The first to arrive after me were Joe and Lisa. Then Denis. The next pair were Brian and Naomi.

Joe brought me a coffee. Starbucks! We chatted. Both Joe and I are on the verge of publishing books on recovery from alcoholism and addiction and we are, well, pretty excited.

Chuck was lugging chairs from the second floor down into the basement. He had taped a sign to the top of the stairwell:

We Are Not Saints
AA Meeting
Downstairs

Next to arrive were Kevin, then Ed, Eric, another Joe, Greg, Jackie, Larry, Julie and Frank.

Joe replaced me as greeter (Larry would take over later) and I went into the church basement to the meeting room. It was small. And it looked like a basement. There was a table with a pew against the wall and then the chairs that Chuck, and now Eric, were lugging down from upstairs. Some people were already sitting in a circle around the table, with a couple of rows on one side. I grabbed a spot on the pew. I hadn't sat on one of those since I was a child. I felt, well, at home. With friends and safe, is how I felt.

More people arrived: Frank, Bob, and Duncan. The last three were Wayne, Dianne and John.

It was 8 PM and Chuck started the meeting, on time. "Good evening," he said. "I want to welcome you to the first meeting of 'We Are Not Saints,' an agnostic AA group in Toronto."

I could feel the pulse of energy in the room. I took another look around the table. Twenty-one people in all: sixteen men and five women. Mid-twenties to mid-sixties. There was a flush of pride on people's faces, a glow in the eyes, a smile on lips. Those present were participating, after all, in a noteworthy event in AA.

As the meeting started, the Minister of the Congregation, Wayne Walder, informally leaned into the room and welcomed those present, a courtesy appreciated by all.

Chuck read the Agnostic AA Preamble:

> *AA agnostic meetings endeavour to maintain a tradition of free expression, and conduct a meeting where alcoholics may feel free to express any doubts or disbeliefs they may have, and to share their own personal form of spiritual experience, their search for it, or their rejection of it. In keeping with AA tradition, we do not endorse or oppose any form of religion or atheism. Our only wish is to ensure suffering alcoholics that they can find sobriety in AA without having to accept anyone else's beliefs, or having to deny their own.*

As is customary at meetings, Lisa then read "What is AA?"

> *Alcoholics Anonymous is a fellowship of men and women who share their experience, strength and hope with each other that they may solve their common problem and help others to recover from alcoholism.*

The only requirement for membership is a desire to stop drinking. There are no dues or fees for AA membership; we are self supporting through our own contributions. AA is not allied with any sect, denomination, politics, organization, or institution; does not wish to engage in any controversy, neither endorses nor opposes any causes. Our primary purpose is to stay sober and help other alcoholics to achieve sobriety.

The respect for privacy at AA meetings, of course, does not allow me to say much more, nor would I wish to. Suffice it to say that the first meeting of the agnostic AA group "We Are Not Saints" was an open meeting and three topics were suggested and discussed, in a lively and engaged fashion, by those present.

The meeting ended, as agnostic meetings invariably do, with the Responsibility Declaration. The adoption of this declaration at AA's 30th anniversary convention in Toronto in 1965 was meant in large part to make AA more inclusive of agnostics and atheists. Bill W, the co-founder of AA, led the way as about 10,000 delegates from 21 different countries held hands and recited it then at Maple Leaf Gardens. Now, on November 30, 2012, almost fifty years later, on a Friday evening in a Unitarian Universalist church basement on Hiawatha Road in downtown Toronto, twenty-one atheists, agnostics and freethinkers held hands and said the declaration together, out loud, reciting it with pride and conviction on that memorable and special occasion: "I am responsible. When anyone anywhere reaches out for help I want the hand of AA always to be there. And for that I am responsible."

As is the case in AA, there was much fellowship after the meeting.

I had a lovely discussion with Duncan, a visitor from a small town in rural Ontario. How did he even hear about the meeting? Turns out Duncan was contemplating starting an agnostic group in his community, and looking for advice and information.

I chatted at some length with Julie. She had once talked at a Beyond Belief meeting of a Mindfulness Based Stress Reduction (MBSR) program she had taken at CAMH and I wanted to know more about it. And my friend, Bob! In the summer (long forgotten now!) he had taught me how to play golf. Bob had come all the way from Whitby in order to show his support to the folks in the room. And I chatted with Eric who had walked by an "old haunt" from his drinking days on his way to the meeting. How his life had changed in AA! And I chatted some more with Joe, first about Bill W, the co-founder of AA, and then about e-readers, like the Kindle, Nook and Kobo.

Oh the fellowship! How I love the fellowship of AA!

Eventually, I made my way back outdoors. A lot of snow had fallen during the meeting. The streets were white. "Winter is here," I thought. I didn't much care though. As I pedaled home, mostly uphill on the way back, there was a celebratory spark in my soul as I contemplated the fact that there were now five agnostic AA groups in the Toronto area. And I was so, so very happy at the thought of next Friday evening's meeting of "We Are Not Saints."

* BK JUST PUBLISHED

* P.140 – SEC AA MTG ROOM

* I'm NOT DIPLOMATIC ENOUGH

'CALL TO ACTION

* WANT NOV 2019 –
ICSAA FEB 2017

News From the Front:
Just listed in S.D. AA Directory
(they wouldn't)

(said: " How else to
better avail ourselves
to the secular AA
commty.

Made in the USA
San Bernardino, CA
20 April 2017